# PRAISE FOR LEADING ORGANIZATIONS FROM THE INSIDE OUT

**Leading Organizations from the Inside Out** *is a great gift to leaders in all three sectors, leading the teams that could transform the enterprise. Action-Learning Teams and After Action Review inspire language and action that can mobilize leaders and teams to build the viable, relevant, and successful organization of the future.*

> **Frances Hesselbein,** Chairman, Leader to Leader Institute

**Leading Organizations from the Inside Out** *gives companies and their leaders critical tools and perspectives that enable them to deal with the fast pace of business in today's world. It offers an especially effective way to initiate change and develop your people at the same time. Don't just read this book...apply its principles.*

> **Bill Owens,** President and CEO, Nortel Networks

*I have had the opportunity to work with small and large organizations. It is amazing to me to see how small organizations work through tough cross-functional issues. In effect, small firms are Action-Learning Teams. Something happens to an organization as it matures. ALTs give way to traditional corporate hierarchy. Medium and large organizations would be well-served to read and adopt the practices outlined in* **Leading Organizations from the Inside Out.** *I know from experience that the practices outlined in this book can positively impact the culture of any organization.*

> **Steve Hooper**, General Partner/Founder, Ignition Partners (Venture Fund)

*Action learning and leading have come of age, thanks in no small part to the authors of this vital book. If the top military and commercial programs are using these concepts to breakthrough traditional barriers, we should all sit up, take notes, and experience excellence in action.*

> **Ken Shelton**, Editor of Leadership Excellence

*Action-Learning Teams built on a foundation of trust, honesty and a dedication to true excellence will soon become the hallmark of all successful organizations. The volatile, uncertain, complex, and ambiguous leadership environment that we all face demands the speed, adaptability, and flexibility that these teams embody.*

> **Major General Robert Ivany**, ret., Former President, U.S. Army War College

*Action-Learning Teams fill the gap between creating the foundations of team dynamics and unleashing talent in a collaborative aligned effort to achieve measurable results. If you need people to work together to solve a problem, improve a process, or create a new product, then this research-based approach provides the "how to" for attaining the best from having people work together.*

**Richard Schuttler,** Center for Advanced Studies, University of Phoenix

*Leading Organizations from the Inside Out is a must read as it clearly articulates solid, user-friendly processes for helping teams create strategic results. As an Executive Coach and former U.S. Navy Test Pilot and squadron commander, my experience is that concepts like Soft-Focus help leaders distinguish what is most important in the midst of complexity, overload and constant change.*

**Linda Shaffer-Vanaria,** President, Enterprise Coaching of Carlsbad

# Leading Organizations from the Inside Out

*Unleashing the Collaborative Genius of Action-Learning Teams*

**Bruce LaRue**
**Paul Childs**
**Kerry Larson**

***Foreword by Marshall Goldsmith***

John Wiley & Sons, Inc.
New York / Chichester / Weinheim / Brisbane / Singapore / Toronto

This book was set in Times New Roman and printed and bound by J & M Reproduction Corporation, Troy, MI. The cover was printed by J & M Reproduction Corporation, Troy, MI.

The paper in this book was manufactured by a mill whose forest management programs include sustained yield harvesting of its timberlands. Sustained yield harvesting principles ensure that the numbers of trees cut each year does not exceed the amount of new growth.

To order books or for customer service, please call 1(800)-CALL-WILEY (225-5945).

ISBN-13   978- 0-471-77167-8
ISBN-10   0-471-77167-8

Printed in the United States of America.

10 9 8 7 6 5 4 3 2 1

# BOOK SYNOPSIS

This innovative book is designed to drastically shorten the time needed to effectively implement change initiatives by helping readers understand both the behavioral and operational aspects of organizational change. The authors demonstrate how, through Action-Learning Teams, organizations can accomplish tangible business objectives while creating superior workforce development. They show leaders how to overcome resistance to change by involving critical stakeholders, including customers, suppliers, and cross-functional teams, in the design and deployment of change initiatives, resulting in drastically shortened time horizons for the successful implementation of change.

# TABLE OF CONTENTS

Bruce LaRue ✧ Paul Childs ✧ Kerry Larson ✧

*The fusion of ever-faster computers with ever-more-reliable telecommunications has spawned creative systems that are already transforming our personal lives, the politics of each of our nations, and the world economy.*

*Information processed by human brainwork into knowledge, integrated and intuited into wisdom has quite suddenly become the world's most important resource...*

*The time is already upon us when symbols, not things, are the world's dominant resource. In consequence we simply cannot keep using, for the management of future complexities, the concepts that seemed to serve us so well in the industrial era that is fast becoming history.*

**Harlan Cleveland**, Former U.S. Ambassador to NATO

# FOREWORD
## *BY MARSHALL GOLDSMITH*

"The leader of the past knew how to *tell*. The leader of the future will know how to *ask*." As a member of the Board of the Peter Drucker Foundation, I had the opportunity to listen to Peter eloquently outline the new world of leadership. He was describing today's world of knowledge workers. Who are knowledge workers? They are people who know more about what they are doing than their managers do! It is hard to *tell* people what to do and how to do it when they already know more than we do. The process involved in Action-Learning Teams (ALT) carries this concept of *asking* to a new level. The ALT model assumes that great knowledge exists in the team and it provides a practical process for tapping into this knowledge. Even more important, ALT helps ensure that the knowledge of the team is translated into action that makes a real difference for the organization.

Many traditional approaches to training and development are like the old approach to leadership. One traditional assumption is that the organization (or the trainer) knows more than the people being trained. Another assumption is that, after people sit in rooms and listen to lectures, they will become enlightened and apply what they have learned on the job – in other words, if we *understand,* we will *do*. In today's fast-paced world, there is very little research to support either one of these assumptions. This is not only easy to see at work, it is easy to see in the broader society. Almost all Americans understand that we should eat a healthy diet and that we should work out. Millions of Americans just don't do it! ALT is a process that requires doing, not just understanding! It recognizes that in Action-Learning, our *understanding* comes from our practice in *doing*.

One common characteristic of high achievers is self-determination. In other words, successful people do what we do because we *choose* to do it – not because we *have to* do it. When we do what we choose to do, we are committed. When we do what we have to do, we are compliant. The impact of personal commitment is true in almost any occupation and can be observed by a small child. Do you remember when you were in grade school? Some teachers were teaching you because they loved teaching. Others were teaching you because they just wanted to collect a check at the end of the month. Even as a child, could you tell the difference? The ALT approach builds upon this concept of commitment. When the idea for change is imposed upon the team, the team is likely to reject the idea. When the idea for change emerges from the team, the team is much more likely to effectively implement the idea.

In my work as an executive coach, I play the role of a facilitator, not an expert. My research (with thousands of respondents) has clearly shown that when leaders ask their coworkers for input, listen to coworkers' ideas, determine what they truly want to change and follow up in a disciplined manner, they almost always become more effective. This is parallel to people who exercise in a disciplined manner and get in great physical condition. Part of my job as a coach is to help leaders learn from their key stakeholders; another part is to help them apply what they are learning on an ongoing basis. While my work involves change at the individual level, Bruce, Paul and Kerry show us how to produce this same type of change at the team level.

The process described in this book is something that almost any organization or team can use. Don't just read it – apply it! Apply it in your own organization and with your own teams. You may be amazed at how quickly this process can make a positive difference.

# PREFACE

## INSPIRATION FOR THIS BOOK

Warren Bennis was finishing a keynote address to a packed audience at the Linkage 2003 Global Institute for Leadership Development (GILD) conference when a man stood to ask him a question: "Dr. Bennis," he asked, " What is the most important thing that leaders today need to know in order to be successful?"

The answer Warren Bennis would give to this open-ended question left us speechless. He said that, in his view, leaders today need to understand action-learning and how to apply this unique form of learning in a team setting. He said that, while we are learning a great deal about how to become leaders, we must do much more to understand how to apply what we know within the complex milieu of the real world with all its political, social, and economic intricacies. While he admitted that he did not fully understand how to do this, he felt that much needed to be done in this area in order for leaders to be successful today.

My colleagues and I had been researching and consulting in the field of Action-Learning for several years, and Dr. Bennis' comments were all we needed to finally motivate us to write this book.

While we wrote the first edition of this book under a nearly impossible four month deadline, we had a chance to completely re-organize and re-write this current Edition. Readers will benefit from extensive feedback we received from students and professionals in a wide range of industries and sectors who have applied the principles in this book. We have also provided many new examples of Action-Learning Teams being used in organizations today.

This being said, we look at this book as a living document that will continue to grow and evolve as it is sharpened and honed in the arena of real-world practice. To this end, we welcome your comments, suggestions, and stories about how you apply what you read here to your own work in organizations.

Bruce LaRue
University Place, Washington

Paul Childs
Oak Park, California

Kerry Larson
Redmond, Washington

# ACKNOWLEDGEMENTS

This book has been a collaborative effort, not only of the three authors, but of a number of key people who contributed to this work.

We would like to give special thanks to Marshall Goldsmith, who contributed the forward and strongly encouraged us to write this book. He has been a great example of someone who makes things happen and is willing to share his tremendous knowledge and experience with those around him.

We would like to thank Richard Schuttler, former Dean of the University of Phoenix Center for Advanced Studies, for his encouragement and insight. We hope to continue our learning about team leadership and Action-Learning from Rich, his colleagues, and students.

We are grateful to Steve Hooper and Bill Owens for their thoughtful input and comments. They are both great leaders that demonstrate many of the principles in this book.

We also thank Kurt Maass for his review and thoughtful suggestions on our early transcripts of this book.  His insights, which stem from many years as a senior executive in the wireless telecom sector, were invaluable to this final product.  We also want to thank Kas Salazar, our editor at John Wiley & Sons, for her suggestions and guidance in writing this book.

Special thanks to Sarah McArthur, editor and founder of SDedit, for editing this new and revised edition of our book, and to Stephanie Galindo for detailed pre-press formatting and contributions to the section on Spiral Dynamics.  We also want to thank Brenda LaRue, who served as copy editor for the first edition of this book.  While we wrote the first edition under a nearly impossible four month deadline, Brenda made us sound like one voice and gave us many suggestions to improve the flow and readability of the book.

We are all deeply grateful to our families whose support and encouragement had a great influence on this book. It is in families that Action-Learning happens on a daily basis.

# INTRODUCTION

## PURPOSE OF THIS BOOK

At one level, this is a guidebook for the design and implementation of organizational change initiatives through the use of Action-Learning Teams (ALT). It is designed to drastically shorten the time needed to effectively implement change initiatives by helping you understand both the behavioral and operational aspects of organizational change.

We demonstrate how, through Action-Learning Teams, organizations can accomplish tangible business objectives while creating superior workforce development. Relevant knowledge is created and applied within the context of real work. We show leaders how to overcome resistance to change by involving critical stakeholders—including customers, suppliers, and cross-functional teams—in the design and deployment of change initiatives, resulting in drastically shortened time horizons for the successful implementation of change.

At yet another level, we are suggesting that Action-Learning can also fundamentally transform organizations by impacting the very culture of an organization. Action-Learning Teams can accomplish this by giving us new approaches and capabilities to deal with the complex and fast-moving environment we find ourselves in today. Action-Learning Teams can help bring your organization closer to becoming a true learning organization by incorporating the habit of "reflection in action" into the fabric of organizational life.

## WHY READ THIS BOOK?

We have seen in the last twenty years a proliferation of management and organizational methodologies, principles, and techniques. We have been introduced to reengineering, total quality, kaizen, empowerment, transformational leadership, networks, alliances, matrix organizations, together with scores of team development processes, all promising to help us cope with the pace of change and complexity found in today's organizations.

Despite all these advances in new thinking and techniques, most organizations today do not look or operate much differently than those of fifty years ago. The control-based hierarchy with its functional divisions, fragmented information, and differentiated roles is still the organization found today. After all the efforts of the last number of years, fundamental transformation is still largely an illusion.

In an article in Fast Company (Webber 2001), Richard Pascale states that we still operate according to three fundamental beliefs about business, emerging from what he called the "social engineering model" of management:

> First, intelligence is located at the top; leadership is the head, organization is the body. Second, change is predictable. That is, when you design a change effort, there is a reasonable degree of predictability and control. Third, there is the assumption of cascading intention: Once a course of action is determined, initiative flows from the top down, and the only trick is to communicate it and roll it out through the ranks.

We agree with Pascale when he goes on to say, "Those three assumptions are deeply baked into the minds of most executives. Those assumptions are so fundamental to how we think about business that it's hard even to be aware of how they govern the way organizations are run."

While many organizations are embarking on initiatives designed to help them cope with the complexity and pace of change, these three assumptions continue to prevail. The results are frustrated leaders, disillusioned workers, and very little lasting change. Many leaders and workers have been through these less-than-optimal change efforts many times and have learned to live with marginal results, since no better choices seem to be available. Yet most recognize that something more needs to be done.

The reason we believe most of these efforts are lacking is that the necessary people who are affected and care about these changes are not included in the assessment, design, and deployment of these changes. We need to engage key stakeholders beyond inviting them to a company meeting to hear what a small executive team came up with about how they are going to do their work differently in the future. It is our experience that organizations managed in this way fail to tap into a hidden reservoir of talent, knowledge and energy that is increasingly necessary to navigate change today. In the pages that follow, we will take you on a profound process of organizational transformation, engaging the critical stakeholders of organizations through what we call Action-Learning Teams.

# NEW APPROACHES TO WORKFORCE DEVELOPMENT AND SUCCESSION PLANNING

The ALT process is designed to enhance current training and development initiatives, as well as your organization's ability to achieve lasting results and commitment to change from its critical stakeholders. This is becoming an issue for many organizations as they emerge from downsizing and streamlining measures that leave them with a core body of essential employees known as knowledge workers. The knowledge workers and executives that remain in the core of today's firms are going to require significant levels of development in order to keep up with the increasing pace of change, heightened competition from the emerging economies of countries like China and India, and the technological complexity emerging in the decades ahead. This is all occurring as the U.S. and many advanced industrialized countries experience a shrinking of their labor force due to the retirement of the baby boom generation. This new demographic reality will continue to challenge organizations to evolve new strategies for developing and retaining the talent they currently possess, while coping with a veritable crisis in succession planning brought about by these demographic changes.

## WHO SHOULD READ THIS BOOK

This book should appeal to anyone who feels that they have outgrown the limitations of their current way of working. Inquisitive executives, human resource practitioners, managers, training and development facilitators, educators, and knowledge workers seeking new avenues of personal and professional development should all benefit from reading this book. The book is practical in focus, using examples taken from the authors' extensive experience and research in order to illustrate how Action-Learning Teams can be used effectively in practice.

## A GLIMPSE AT THE ROAD AHEAD

In Part I, we define Action-Learning Teams and demonstrate how to successfully lead these teams in the design and deployment of initiatives intended to move your organization forward. The process we describe is based on a careful analysis of how we have witnessed and worked with organizations using Action-Learning Teams successfully. Our aim is to bring these principles to the surface in order to allow organizations to adapt these principles to their own unique situation.

We integrate both behavioral and operational dimensions of team development within four key phases of the change process: *Inquiry, Design, Deployment*, and *Integration*. We also describe the different forms of leadership that are most appropriate for each phase of the change process.

In Part II of this book, we describe the context that has given rise to these teams and how to identify where they may be currently operating "below the radar" in your organization. We discuss several examples of how these teams are being used in practice. We also describe how, with proper stewardship, these teams can help develop the fundamental competencies necessary for leading the knowledge-intensive organization of the 21st century.

In Part III, we will supply you with the fundamental concepts underlying Action-Learning: key research, the origin of Action-Learning as a discipline, and the use of Action-Learning Teams in distributed organizations and online learning environments.

# PART I

# THE DESIGN AND DEPLOYMENT OF STRATEGIC CHANGE

In this section, we will define **Action-Learning Teams** (ALTs) and explore an Action-Learning process designed for addressing major issues within an organization utilizing cross-functional Action-Learning Teams. We will investigate both behavioral and operational dimensions of this process, as well as the leadership characteristics most appropriate for each phase of a major change initiative.

This process has proven to be a very effective method for creating significant and lasting organizational change. This experience has also been invaluable for ALT participants in the development of their leadership skills, especially effective team leadership and leading complex change efforts. This last point is important as organizations are increasingly seeking effective ways to develop their key people and increase their bench strength for the future.

# 1 GETTING STARTED

## WHAT ARE ACTION-LEARNING TEAMS?

Action-Learning Teams (ALTs) are a unique form of team charged with developing specialized capabilities that do not currently exist in the organization. These capabilities are designed to close particular process gaps, or to generate new capacity for the organization where none had existed before. The capabilities developed by Action-Learning Teams tend to be strategic in nature, and of a form not readily developed by other means such as formal education or training. Action-Learning Teams tend by nature to be cross-functional and even cross-organizational, drawing together individuals with highly specialized knowledge in order to collaborate on the development and application of new forms of knowledge. Action-Learning Teams rely on a particular form of learning characterized by reflection in action, and the capabilities they develop are created by a form of intellectual boot-strapping wherein new knowledge and capacity are created that did not exist before.

We have all heard the saying, "Experience is the best teacher." Yet relying on experience alone leaves us vulnerable to continually reinventing the wheel and repeating yesterday's mistakes. As the pace of change quickens, we find ourselves reacting to problems and feeling that we don't have the luxury of formulating a more thoughtful response to our situation. We may feel that we need to update our skills and knowledge, but the occasional weekend seminar or conference seems ill-suited to help us cope with the complexities we face on a daily basis.

Many have responded in these circumstances by returning to the university classroom to earn new credentials. Yet, in many important respects, the distance between the traditional university classroom and the shop floor has never been wider (Task Force on High-Performance Work and Workers 1997).

What we need today is relevant knowledge in a form that we can rapidly apply, test, and refine within our current context (LaRue 2002). Individuals and groups at all levels of the organization must also learn to apply this knowledge in a manner that explicitly aligns with the strategic direction of the organization. Under these circumstances, we find that the knowledge we need is often so context-sensitive and unique to the complexities of the task at hand that our peers are the best source of knowledge and insight. However, the dynamics of many teams and the results they achieve too often leave us wanting. The paradox of organizations today is that we can accomplish little of significance alone, yet many groups and whole organizations simply do not function well, and at their worst can be a drain to the human spirit.

Organizations today are also characterized by the non-routine: unforeseen problems and opportunities being the order of the day. As Peter Drucker (1999; 2002) is fond of pointing out, we must learn to exploit the opportunities that may not have been part of official strategy. In addition, we must learn to abandon tried and true but outmoded practices in order to free up resources to exploit these opportunities.

Increasingly, it is workers at the periphery of the organization who are able to spot these hidden opportunities, and it is therefore critical that the organization remain flexible enough to respond accordingly. As we will see, Action-Learning Teams are a highly flexible means of organizing that enables organizations to seize upon the unexpected.

The concept of Action-Learning Teams emerged less from a desire to invent a new form of team and more from the observation, research, and experience of ourselves and others as to how the most successful groups perform under pressure to create extraordinary results. Our goal in this book is to learn from these examples and distill the basic principles that make these groups successful. We then attempt in Part II to create a systematic approach wherein teams can consciously use these principles to achieve breakthrough results. Further, our goal is to help executives and managers realize the larger potential inherent in Action-Learning Teams to create a culture that fosters innovation.

# STAGES OF THE ACTION-LEARNING TEAM PROCESS

We have broken out the process of Action-Learning into four parts. While these parts define the Action-Learning stages, they are not set in stone. Some teams may go through all the stages, others may have already progressed within the ALT development process, and still others may bypass certain stages altogether. The stages are:

1. Inquiry
2. Design
3. Deployment
4. Integration

**Inquiry** is a deep and incisive discovery process that illuminates the specific gaps in the organization, reveals how they are measured, and directs the focus of the ALT. Inquiry reveals the blind spots: the areas of gaps in knowledge, understanding, and process that have created dysfunctional patterns of behavior. Inquiry is about understanding where to put your organizational crowbar in order to obtain the maximum amount of leverage.

Inquiry is a disciplined process designed to systematically expose and question the basic assumptions about organizational reality (Bohm 1994; Bohm and Nichol 1996; Kegan and Lahey 2001). It is a focused questioning that requires organizations and individuals to examine the paradigms and models that limit their thinking.

**Design** is a process that explores how to create a road map for true innovative change. This is the blueprint of how to bridge the gaps uncovered in the Inquiry phase. It makes use of brainstorming with a team in a specific way that will generate new ways of thinking and break the old patterns of creating solutions from within the same "box" from which the problem was derived.

This process engages the key stakeholders as well as the end user, the customer or the client in the creation of that solution. Design explores the concept of piloting a project whenever possible and testing the design before deploying it throughout the organization.

**Deployment** examines how to break the barriers that typically impede change in an organization. It explores how teams can create common interests and deploy their chosen initiatives with speed and power. Deployment begins to change the fixed identities that organizations establish for themselves. It examines how to overcome common resistance to change such as *complacency,* which arises in highly controlled environments or organizations that are over-managed. It attacks the *self dramatization* that causes companies to resist change, continuing their collective stories about how they are *victims* of management, or the organization, or even the marketplace. Engaging in the proper method of deployment breaks the illusion of powerlessness that creates resistance to change.

**Integration** is designed to synthesize lessons learned and make them a part of the organization's DNA by deploying short-term wins, engaging reluctant managers, and ensuring that the change initiatives become woven into the fabric of the entire company. The process of integration helps create new norms and shared values throughout the organization that reinforce the new initiatives by systematically reshaping organizational culture. Integration, when done properly, becomes a permanent new and empowering way for those in the organization to view themselves and the outside world by engaging customers and other critical stakeholders in the constant evolution of new solutions.

# WHEN IS AN ACTION-LEARNING TEAM APPROPRIATE?

An ALT can be very effective when addressing key organizational issues under the right circumstances. Several considerations should be weighed when deciding whether an organizational issue lends itself to an Action-Learning approach or not.

Does the organization view the issue as important enough to apply the necessary resources (time, money, and effort) of an ALT? The ALT should not be used on minor issues that don't warrant the focus and attention of senior management. When ALTs are applied to such minor issues as how high the cubicles should be or how much should we charge for soft drinks, team members will feel their time is being wasted and will trivialize the Action-Learning process.

Can the issue be addressed and improved within the organization? An ALT will work when addressing an issue that is within the control of the organization and/or can be improved by the efforts and actions of the team. Issues such as the economic climate or government laws and regulations are examples of some things an organization will not have much power over. However, the organization does have control over *how* they will respond to outside events or changes. Action-Learning Teams can be utilized to address *how* the organization will deal with changes in laws or regulations, *how* the organization will respond to the impact of a downturn in the economic climate, or *how* it will cope with any other significant event, such as a merger/acquisition, major shift in strategy, and the like.

Does the organization have the necessary expertise internally to apply to the issue?

An ALT should be made up of individuals who have the necessary knowledge, experience, and skills to address the issue, understand the root causes, and are able to design and implement possible solutions. However, an ALT is not appropriate when the necessary knowledge and expertise is not available within the organization, or if it would be difficult to obtain the knowledge necessary to create a viable solution.

Will the issue have sufficient involvement and support from the key functions or groups of the organization?

The success of an ALT is predicated on the represented involvement of key groups and the support of the management of those groups. It will be a frustrating experience for an ALT if key groups aren't willing to be involved or support the effort.

Will the ALT have necessary ability and freedom to investigate the issue, find the causes, design, and implement creative solutions?

For an ALT to be successful, it needs to have a relatively free hand to carry out its assignment. If management already has decided how to solve the issue or the direction it should go, then an ALT will experience a great deal of frustration and may be counter-productive in the long run. It is important for an ALT to discuss expectations with management early on to clarify how much freedom it has to address the issue.

If the answer to any of the above questions is "no", then an ALT may not be the appropriate method of addressing the issue. Action-Learning Teams are not the only means for organizations to address issues or problems. Organizations may form a committee, establish a task force or cross-functional team, or have an executive or group of executives address the issue and propose a solution. These other forms may be more appropriate given the circumstances and political climate of the organization. However, the ALT, given the right circumstances, is a very powerful method for effective organizational change and leadership development.

# THE FORMATION OF AN ACTION-LEARNING TEAM

The initial step in putting together an ALT that will direct a major change effort is to find the right membership. Five **key characteristics** are essential to effective Action-Learning Teams. They are:

1. **Experience/Expertise**: The team needs to have the relevant points of view represented – functions, work experience, key customers and suppliers, etc. – relative to the issue at hand so that informed, intelligent decisions will be made.

2. **Respect:** The team members need to have the credibility in the organization so that the results and recommendations will be taken seriously by all parts of the organization.

3. **Key Positions:** The team should include enough players who have position power so that those not included on the ALT will not easily block progress.

4. **Leadership:** The team needs to have proven leaders able to make things happen and drive the change process in the organization.

5. **Team Players:** The members of the team should have the reputation and history of working effectively on a team – having more of a 'we' rather than an 'I' attitude.

There are certain types of people who should not be included on an Action-Learning Team. One is the person that has a huge ego, who wants all the attention, and leaves no room for anyone else. These people usually have high control needs and want to direct others and make decisions. Key leaders in organizations usually have strong egos, and unless they are keenly aware of their own limitations, appreciate other members' strengths, and have the ability to focus on the greater goal of the team rather than their short-term interests, they should not be included on an ALT.

Another type of person to avoid is the one who develops mistrust on a team and kills the possibility of effective teamwork. They are the ones who undermine individual team members or the team as a whole by telling some people on the team about other members behind their backs, thereby negatively affecting the relationships of individuals on the team. They are disastrous to the necessary trust for effective teamwork.

The third type of individual to be concerned about is the minimally committed individual. Being a member of an ALT takes a high degree of energy and commitment. Those that are reluctant to join when asked should not be on the team.

The three ingredients to a successful ALT are: 1) having the right people on the team, 2) having a shared common goal, and 3) creating a high level of trust among team members.

# CHARACTERISTICS OF AN ACTION-LEARNING TEAM LEADER

The characteristics of an ALT leader are a combination of business resolve and the ability to effectively facilitate a team to get positive results. Depending on the culture of the organization, they may also need to have position power to have access to and influence on the rest of the organization.

**Characteristics** of an ALT leader/facilitator:

- High level of trust and respect by and for the team
- Very confident of self and open to feedback and criticism
- Flexible - able to adapt their facilitation style to the needs of the team

- Able to build a team culture around the idea of freedom and responsibility
- Thinks in terms of 'we' instead of 'I'
- Has high standards – doesn't tolerate mediocrity in self or others
- Results-oriented – a catalyst in producing great results
- Possesses determination – does whatever it takes to get the job done
- Great advocate of ALT to the organization

The following are the **skills or competencies** of an ALT leader or facilitator in order of importance as perceived by experienced group facilitators (Rothwell 1999):

1. Listens actively for thoughts and feelings
2. Questions effectively to evoke team thinking and action
3. Good observer of behavior of individuals and the dynamics of the group
4. Stimulates group insights
5. Focuses group attention on the appropriate issue
6. Able to paraphrase for understanding by all
7. Observes body language of participants
8. Able to summarize large amounts of information generated by the team
9. Uses body language and nonverbal communication
10. Ability to focus the team's attention on the key issues
11. Able to articulate own thoughts and feelings without undue influence on the team
12. Able to direct the team's thinking on an issue or topic

We suggest also, whenever possible, that the ALT leader have prior experience as a member of an ALT.

# CREATING EFFECTIVE ACTION-LEARNING TEAMS

The leader of an ALT has the responsibility of making sure the team is operating at its optimal level and that all members are working to improve their participation. The challenge to the leader is how to build effective teams in an environment of rapid change and with limited time and resources. When needed, we suggest the following team-building process that is highly focused, includes disciplined feedback and follow-up, doesn't waste time and has participants focus on self-improvement. Marshall Goldsmith, the creator of this tool, calls the process outlined below "Team Building Without Time Wasting" (Goldsmith, Lyons et al. 2000, adapted with permission).

Research involving thousands of participants (Hesselbein, Goldsmith et al. 1996; Carter, Giber et al. 2000; Fulmer and Goldsmith 2001; Segil, Goldsmith et al. 2003) has shown how focused feedback and follow-up can increase leadership and customer service effectiveness. This parallel approach to team building by Marshall Goldsmith has been shown to help leaders build teamwork without requiring a lot of time. While the approach is simple, it does require that team members have the courage to ask for suggestions, the discipline to develop a behavioral change strategy, and to systematically follow through on their specific commitment to change.

The team leader will need to assume the role of coach or facilitator, and fight the urge to be the "boss" of the project. Greater improvement in teamwork will generally occur if the team members develop their own behavioral change strategy than will occur if the leader develops the strategy and imposes it on the team. The following are the **steps in the process**:

1.  Ask each member of the team to answer two questions: a) "On a 1-10 scale, how well are we doing in terms of working together as a team?" and b) "On the same scale, how well do

we need to be doing in terms of working together as a team?" After the results are calculated, discuss as a team the gap between current effectiveness and desired effectiveness and the need for improved teamwork.

2. Ask the team, "If *every* team member could change two key behaviors that would help us close the gap between *where we are* and *where we want to be*, which two behaviors should we all try to change as a team?" Have each team member record the selected behaviors and then put them on flip charts.

3. Have the team members prioritize all the behaviors on the charts and determine the one or two most important behaviors for all team members to change.

4. Ask each team member to have a one-on-one dialogue (about five minutes each) with each other team member. During the dialogue, each member will request that their colleague suggest two areas for their personal behavioral change in the future (other than the one or two already agreed upon for every team member) that will help the team close the gap between *where we are* and *where we want to be*. Team members should be encouraged to *listen* to all suggestions without judgment or criticism of the feedback.

5. Now have each team member review their list of suggested changes and select the two that seem to be the most important to them. Then each team member should announce his or her one or two key behaviors for personal change to the team.

6. Encourage each team member to ask for a brief (five minute), monthly progress report from each other team member on their effectiveness in demonstrating the one or two key behaviors common to all team members and the one or two key personal behaviors. Specific suggestions for improvement can be solicited in areas where behavior does not match desired expectations.

7. We suggest that, after a period of time, a mini-survey follow-up process be conducted. This individual survey will include the two common items and the two personal items of each member. They are simple enough to be put on a postcard. Then have team members calculate the results for

themselves. They don't need to discuss their "numbers" with the group – only what they have learned.

8. In a team meeting, have each team member discuss key learning points from their mini-survey results and ask for further suggestions in a brief one-on-one dialogue with each other team member. The leader then facilitates a discussion on how the team is doing in terms of increasing its effectiveness in the two key behaviors that were selected for all team members. Provide the team with positive recognition for increased effectiveness in teamwork. Encourage team members to keep focused on increasing their effectiveness in demonstrating the behaviors that they are trying to improve.

The process described above works well with ALTs or any team because it is highly focused, includes disciplined feedback and follow-up, does not waste time, and causes participants to focus on self-improvement. The process also works because it provides ongoing suggestions and reinforcement. Any research on behavioral change will show that feedback and reinforcement for new behavior needs to occur on a frequent basis.

A final reason that the process works is because it encourages participants to focus on self-improvement. Many team-building processes degenerate because team members are primarily focused on solving *someone else's* problems. This process works because it encourages team members to primarily focus on solving *their own* problems!

# 2 INQUIRY - DISCOVERING THE GAPS THAT IMPEDE EFFECTIVENESS

## PURPOSE

Too often individuals lack a keen sense of the systems in which they operate and of the powerful internal and external forces that shape their world. Leaders must continually look outside of their organizations to gain a deeper understanding of those forces operating in the society and economy that will have an impact on their company.

Inquiry is a process that examines and observes the organizational strategy in light of the major forces driving change in the environment, whether internal or external. It ensures that the appropriate competencies, systems, and processes will be implemented to accomplish this strategy. Inquiry is a discovery process that illuminates specific gaps in the organization, reveals how they are measured, and directs the focus of the Action-Learning Team.

Inquiry tests assumptions and reveals blind spots and gaps in knowledge, beliefs, and processes that have created dysfunctional patterns of behavior. Precise inquiry reveals the organizational "filters" through which the external world is seen. Ultimately, inquiry helps us understand where to put our "organizational crowbar" in order to obtain the maximum amount of leverage for our efforts.

The process of inquiry is therefore a critical phase that must be executed successfully prior to designing a major change initiative. Often, organizations do not change in the absence of a crisis. Inquiry is the process that sets the stage for pioneering change in the absence of a crisis. If change of this nature is not managed properly, the organization could emerge worse off than when it started the process. Such failure is often not the result of the proposed changes themselves, but rather the management of the context into which these changes are introduced.

# THE ROLE OF ASSUMPTIONS, CONTEXT, AND CULTURE

Examples abound of companies that operated on a certain set of assumptions that blinded them to new opportunities and challenges that did not fit within their current frame of reference.

For example, in the mid 1990s, Microsoft under Bill Gates leadership *saw themselves* as a stand-alone software company; their core strategy was to duplicate Microsoft software on as many personal computers in the world as possible. Given this lens through which Microsoft saw the world and their role within it, they did not recognize the opportunity/threat represented by the Internet and the browser market in particular. All of this was about to change as Microsoft re-examined and then rapidly changed their operating assumptions to include the Internet.

At the time, Netscape™ dominated the browser world with more than 80% of the market. Most users simply preferred to use Netscape™ over Internet Explorer™ or other Web browsers such as Mosaic™, Lynx™ and Opera™. In the summer of 1996, Microsoft released Internet Explorer 3.0™, which seemingly overnight launched Explorer to the top of the browser market and relegated Netscape™ to an also-ran. The Internet was now *integrated* into its operating system—as well as the operating assumptions that governed how Microsoft ran their company. Today, Microsoft's Internet Explorer™ has a global usage share of 95 percent as reported by *OneStat.com*.

In yet another example, although the Xerox Palo Alto Research Center (PARC) was a computing think tank where brilliant minds innovated on a routine basis, even they did not understand the potential of the graphical user interface technology they had created. Steve Jobs, operating from a different set of assumptions, recognized the potential immediately and understood how to capitalize on the new technology—and the rest, as they say, is history. As Steve Wozniak says on his Web site (*www.woz.org*), "Steve Jobs made the case to Xerox PARC executives directly that they had great technology but that Apple knew how to make it affordable enough to change the world..."

Bell Labs obviously had no idea about the potential of their single most important invention: the transistor. While they saw some use for the transistor in telecommunications, they practically gave away the technology, and now the transistor serves as the foundation for nearly every electronics company in the world.

The key point for leaders to understand here is that some of the most potent opportunities for innovation are right before our eyes. But why are companies so often incapable of recognizing what is right in front of them? The problems are the assumptions, filters, and beliefs about our products and services, and our preconceptions about our customers' needs and how they will use our products.

In short, as leaders we must become expert at creating a context conducive to innovation, for it is this context that shapes our beliefs in the organization about what is possible. The problem is in the fact that context, like culture, is ubiquitous, taken for granted, and transparent. As such, context is as powerful as it is illusive and difficult to change.

Inquiry is the process of discovering context and making it visible, and thus amenable to change. In this way, individuals, teams, and entire organizations can understand and judge the appropriateness of their strategies and subsequent actions. In organizations, the main source of context is culture: the beliefs, values and world views that are imbedded in the company largely through its history and leadership.

Like water to the fish, culture in its most fundamental sense is so all-pervasive that it becomes transparent to those who live within it. It is often only when we visit a culture as an outsider, or if we confront a crisis that forces us to re-evaluate our situation, that we can actually become aware of the norms, values, and assumptions that govern the behavior of the people operating within that context. Culture in this sense becomes, in effect, a collective trance. That is, when a group or entire organization shares a certain set of taken-for-granted assumptions and beliefs, they are to this degree constrained from creating novel alternatives and approaches. In short, they are unable to innovate and create fundamental change for themselves and their customers. Inquiry is designed to help members of an organization understand their own culture and how that culture impacts daily operations and decisions.

## THE BELIEF MODEL

Aldous Huxley proposed that one of the primary functions of the human brain is to regulate the amount of information we have to process in our ordinary waking consciousness. The metaphor he employed is the reducing valve. In his view, the business of the brain is to keep from becoming overwhelmed and confused by the flood of sensory information from the environment and the memories of past associations that prevent us from focusing on immediate survival demands.

People, groups, and entire organizations often find ingenious ways of slowing down the rate of change. This is a reaction to feeling overwhelmed, overloaded, and confused. Too much change yields too many problems. This creates the necessity for more solutions, yet often these solutions are in the form of reactions that keep us busy treating symptoms rather than eliminating the underlying cause of the problems we face.

These tactics are the present day's reducing valve. All of them are designed to allow people to cope, but all of them remove us from the present moment and prevent us from solving the underlying problem at hand. The danger is that, by staying here too long, we create a strong set of beliefs that shape our reality.

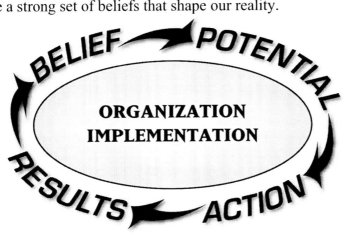

*Figure 1: The Belief Model—This model demonstrates how limiting beliefs can eventually lead to limited results.*

As teams create a strong set of beliefs, these beliefs are reinforced as an endless loop. If they have limited beliefs about themselves, they have limited potential. With limited potential, they take very little action to change. With limited action, they get very limited results that *reinforce* the limited beliefs with which they began the entire process.

# RECOGNIZING PATTERNS

During any initiative or event, teams create two levels of reality: what actually happens and their interpretation and beliefs about what happens. It is through the filter of these beliefs that behaviors are unconsciously shaped, and these beliefs guide the team's subsequent actions.

Once team members begin to recognize the context of how they are viewing a problem, a sense of *pattern recognition* begins to emerge. At first, this pattern recognition may occur at a purely cognitive level. We notice the pattern of our thoughts, the pattern of how we feel, and finally the patterns of our actions or behaviors borne out of these thoughts and beliefs. However, it is critical that participants recognize these patterns as such, and *do not personalize the patterns they discover.* A common manifestation of personalization is blame, guilt, becoming a victim or finger-pointing.

Personalization makes individuals feel victimized and somehow unaccountable for the results they create in the organization (Kegan and Lahey 2001). This victim mentality is a common dysfunctional pattern of individual, team, and/or company behavior. It is a means of avoiding personal accountability and responsibility for change.

# LEADERSHIP ASSESSMENT

We recommend that all key members of the ALT undergo a 360 multi-source feedback (MSF) assessment. These assessment instruments are becoming commonplace in many organizations, and consist of a systematic feedback process involving a cross-section of *stakeholders,* including one's boss, peers, and subordinates. We also like to include feedback from key vendors, suppliers, and customers in this feedback process. Results of this feedback should be used as a development tool only, and should not be used in any way for formal evaluation purposes. This helps ensure that the feedback one receives is honest and straightforward.

Once MSF reports are generated, it is important for each individual receiving feedback to debrief their results with a trained coach or other qualified professional. The coach helps to identify key strengths and areas for improvement, and helps create a development plan. The coach also prepares the individual to follow up systematically with their stakeholder group, informing them of their development goals and gathering specific suggestions for improvement to be acted upon.

Development goals should whenever possible be targeted at specific behaviors and be in alignment with the strategic direction of the organization. The key to this entire process is for individuals receiving feedback to consistently follow up with their stakeholders and to visibly act on their suggestions for improvement. This process in effect turns one's stakeholder group into a team of coaches. No one knows us better than those with whom we work most closely. If we can learn to give and receive feedback more as a gift than as criticism, we can continue to evolve and grow as individuals and as team members.

# THE PIP PROCESS

The key to the Inquiry process is to discover the key issues that reside in the organization and then to recognize the patterns and beliefs that underlie these issues. A powerful tool that can be used to discover the core issues is something called PIP, or Potential Improvement Points, a process originally created by Dr. Ichak Adizes (1999) of the Adizes Institute in Santa Barbara, California. The PIP process is nothing more than a way to get to the core issues that underlie the key problems in an organization so they can be solved.

We have found that the most productive means of engaging in this process is through an off-site meeting. While it is not mandatory to hold this meeting off-site, we highly recommend this approach. These meetings are a way to collectively propel the team forward, share common knowledge and create a bond around a critical theme or issue. The meeting should have a minimum of 10 people and no more than 30. This meeting is not necessarily composed merely of members of the Action-Learning Team, but should include a cross-section of senior management who will need to support the process. Whenever possible, the meeting should also include key vendors, business partners and customers.

## KEY QUESTIONS TO ASK

Inquiry is conducted by asking key questions, which are designed to forward the discovery process. Questions include:

- *What behaviors are truly rewarded in your company? Which behaviors go unrewarded or are punished?*

When you take a good look at what is truly rewarded in your company, you may find that it is behaviors such as covering for others' mistakes, maintaining the status quo at any price, and simply showing up for work. If the company or team is run by an administrator, rewards might be for following the rules, procedures, and formal policies.

- *What is working now? What specifically could be improved?*

Focus first on what is working now. Organizations and teams continually focus on what *isn't* working. A collective mind-set can develop if teams continually talk about their problems without focusing on creating substantive solutions. This can lead to a condition of learned helplessness. Teams can become victims of their own circumstances. While it is essential that we ask ourselves the hard questions, begin by asking, *"What is working well now?"*

This creates momentum that will allow the team to focus on the next question: *"What can be improved?"* Don't ask simply, *"What's wrong?"* or *"What's broken?"* or *"What's wrong with them?"* Questions such as these tend to personalize the issues and keep the inquiry from being open for reflection and observation. Participants may become defensive, which can halt the inquiry before it has even begun.

- ### How is knowledge created and transferred in your organization?

Is knowledge created and transferred in a collaborative, cross-functional, and flexible manner? Is knowledge gained by continuous questioning, ad hoc teams, and bypassing the current system? Or is it hierarchical, rigid, and limited to specific teams, departments, and individuals? Is knowledge shared or is it contained and protected within organizational silos? People who are true knowledge seekers tend to think outside the box and take more risks. They tend to learn quickly and adapt their learning to the problem at hand. They tend to think in terms of systems and cross-functional processes, rather than being oriented around functions or organizational silos.

- ### What are the cultural dynamics that develop and transfer this knowledge?

How do teams work together? Is knowledge transferred across functional lines based on the needs of the immediate problem? Quite often, cultural diversity in organizations emerges in the form of a conflict of style or conflict of interest. These conflicts can impede the development or transfer of new knowledge. All teams have conflict at one time or another, but sometimes the conflict can be destructive. Is there an atmosphere of mutual respect where all sides are being heard? When it comes time to implement or transfer knowledge, does the team share common interests, or do the conflicting interests of the team members keep the new learning from being applied?

- *How is change effected in your organization?*

To create change in an organization, one must understand the root causes of dysfunction or one will merely be treating the symptoms of the disease rather than its cause. Does the leadership of your organization react to circumstances and changes in the market environment, or do they promote a culture that drives and creates change? How is change implemented: is it top-down or highly participatory? Are those most affected by the change also involved in its design and implementation?

## STRUCTURING THE PIP PROCESS

- Place the participants in small groups of no more than six to eight people. The teams should be composed of people who don't normally work together. This is important for the development of cross-functional knowledge transfer. The entire meeting should be conducted in these small teams. This will accelerate the process and allow people to discover how to work in teams.
- Collect the PIPs, or Potential Improvement Points, commonly referred to as problems. Figure 2 describes how Dr. Ichak Adizes (1999) defines a PIP:

  1. Something that is wanted and expected is *not* a PIP.
  2. Something not wanted and expected is a PIP.
  3. Something wanted and unexpected is a PIP.
  4. Something not wanted and unexpected is a PIP.

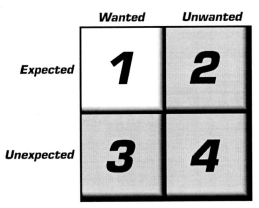

*Figure 2: Defining Potential Improvement Points (PIPs)*

- This should be an information gathering process, not an evaluation process. It is a discovery of the brutal facts of the situation. Collecting (and later sorting and categorizing) the PIPs begin to create context for the problem. The PIPs should be gathered on index cards, with only one PIP per note, without offering any solutions. Avoid stories or explanations about the problems; just simply collect the data.
- As a large group, sort the PIPs by category of problem (see "Sorting the PIPs" later in this chapter). This process helps discover where the focus of the initiative should be based on the weighted results of the accumulation of PIPs.
- After accumulation and sorting of the PIPs, ask questions to prioritize which areas are the most critical to focus on based on the current strategic direction of the company.
- Ask the key questions of the teams (see the following key questions). Allow them to brainstorm as a group. The facilitator should guide, not direct this process. Encourage the team to notice the process they are engaged in as much as the outcomes they discover.
- Initiate a critical discussion about the gaps the group perceives in the organization.

In order to understand an organization's patterns of behavior it is necessary to first classify the PIPs into categories. The facilitator should perform this categorizing process with the participation of the whole group. By engaging in this process, the group will begin to recognize the underlying patterns giving rise to specific problems.

The PIPs in the innermost ring are at the core of the *identity* of the organization. They are the root improvement points that have to do with identity of the company which, if not handled, create other issues in the chain of causality which spread from the innermost rings to the outer rings. Issues of identity can therefore impact issues of *strategy,* which can create issues of *function,* which in turn lead to ineffective behaviors.

# Potential Improvement Points Attributes

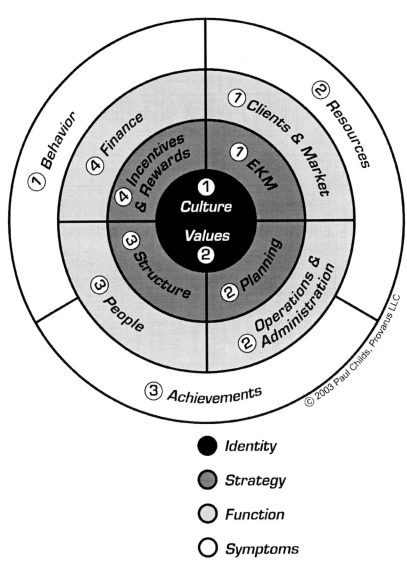

Figure 3: Sorting Potential Improvement Points (PIPs)

# SYMPTOMS

**A-1 Dysfunctional Patterns/Behaviors** – Organizations as well as people can develop dysfunctional patterns of behavior. These behaviors are damaging to the organization and are caused by the PIPs within the inner circles. This is behavior that has not yet taken hold on the culture of the organization. Some examples of dysfunctional behaviors are:

- High turnover
- Poor teamwork
- Bottlenecks cause by people or groups
- Power plays

**A-2 Resources** – These PIPs are a result of wasting or poor utilization of resources. These are manifested as inefficiencies in the organization such as:

- Too much overhead
- Too few resources
- Costs are too high
- Profit is substandard

**A-3 Achievements** – These PIPs reflect the failure of the organization to achieve their outcomes. They are all caused by other areas within the circles. They include:

- Declining market share
- Loss of sales
- Eroding customer base
- No brand loyalty
- Failure to penetrate the market

# FUNCTIONS

**B-1 Clients and Market** – PIPs are grouped into this area if they describe results or processes relating to how the organization communicates with the client. This is where the organization identifies the needs of the client and how the organization can meet those needs. These PIPs usually relate to advertising, public relations, sales, and marketing. They include:

- Poor customer service
- Unclear brand definition
- Ambiguous marketing message
- Poor marketing materials
- Poor Web site performance
- Out of touch with customers
- Unable to anticipate customer needs and market trends

**B-2 Operations and Administration** – These PIPs relate to how the organization provides the products or services the clients want. This area is comprised of how the company transforms inputs into outputs for the customers. This is how the company takes in information and puts out products or services. This includes all operational and administrative elements such as:

- Missed delivery dates
- Poor handling of materials
- Low inventory turns
- Inaccurate orders

**B-3 People** – People are an organization's most critical resource. The PIPs in this area deal with how well the organization treats its people. This covers all areas of Human Resources, training, motivation and compensation including:

- No training for sales team
- No clear leadership track

- No clear succession planning
- No clear paths for development for different areas of the company
- Not taking care of employees
- Compensation and rewards not aligned with strategic priorities

**B-4 Finances** – These PIPs deal with money, financing, and accounting: how we acquire money, use it and account for the finances of the organization, including:

- Faulty credit policy
- Low turnover of receivables
- High payables
- Lack of financial transparency or accountability
- Unethical or questionable accounting practices

# STRATEGY

**C-1 EKM - Enterprise Knowledge Management** – These PIPs are concerned with where key company information resides and how it flows throughout the organization. This includes the management information flow, knowledge management and the ongoing development of organizational intelligence. These PIPs determine whether or not the proper information and intelligence is available to make good management decisions. These PIPs typically relate to the executive or management team and deal with issues such as:

- Uncertainty as to how market intelligence is acquired
- Acquired knowledge may not be relevant
- Inability to create and transfer knowledge effectively throughout the organization
- Management is unwilling to confront the data

- There is little true understanding of customers and their needs
- Organization not staying abreast of relevant developments that may impact the business
- Management being *driven* by change instead of *driving* the change
- Unable to translate data and information into actionable knowledge

**C-2 Planning** – These PIPs deal with the organization's mission, vision and planning process. They include:

- Accomplishing our strategy: Do we have a solid and actionable means of carrying out our strategy? Is our strategy appropriate for today?
- Living our values: Who do we have to be as an organization in order to realize our vision?
- Living the mission: How will we accomplish our mission? What steps do we need to take to make this mission a reality?
- Living the vision: What is the grand dream we would have for ourselves if we had no limits?

**C-3 Structure** – These PIPs relate to organizational structure including the allocation of roles and responsibilities in each department and division, and any functions or jobs that may be missing, including:

- Roles and Responsibilities
  - o Poor job descriptions
  - o Job descriptions too restrictive or inflexible
  - o No one responsible for training and development
- Authority – PIPs that deal with the question of who has authority to decide what, and whether or not authority is centralized or decentralized.
  - o Poor delegation
  - o No one can determine pricing
  - o Split authority in decision-making

**C-4 Incentive and Rewards** – These PIPs focus on the incentives and reward systems that motivate behavior, including:

- Incentives not connected to organization's goals
- Organization competing against itself
- Inequitable commission structure
- Incentives do not support new strategy or change initiative

# CULTURE AND VALUES

**D-1 Culture** – These are the PIPs that describe the shared values or beliefs held by the owners, key leaders or executives, or anyone who has a strong influence on the entire organization. Such attitudes are typically brought into the company from the outside and are the result of the individuals' past experience, education, personal norms and values, etc. If the people with these attitudes were to leave the company, these PIPs would probably go with them. These PIPs may include:

- Dysfunctional leadership style
  o Control issues
  o Narcissistic tendencies
- Paternalism
- Managing by doing or micromanaging
- Lack of vision and strategy
- Poor response to external events that impact the company
- Reacts to rather than driving change

**D-2 Values** – These PIPs involve the value systems and ways of behaving that are pervasive throughout the company. When someone new joins the organization, they describe the environment that exists in the company. They quickly adapt their behavior to fit in, or become affected by these values. Such values may include:

- Lack of clear values in the organization

- Unethical conduct
- Accepting mediocrity
- Power plays and fiefdoms
- Us vs. Them attitude
- Every person for themselves

Be aware that there are also PIPs that may come up in the inquiry that are *not* controllable by the organization. These should not be part of the collection process, but should be set aside since the focus of the inquiry is what the team or the organization can do *that is under their control.* There are no actionable initiatives unless the organization has the power over the PIPs.

# LEADERSHIP DURING INQUIRY

Leading an Action-Learning Team requires a high degree of awareness. The leader needs to be aware of the team dynamics as they form an effective ALT, as well as understand how to keep the team *grounded in reality* as they try to understand the root causes of the issue presented. Leadership skills during this phase include:

- Inquiry is to feed forward, not feedback (Goldsmith 2003; Goldsmith, Morgan et al. 2004). Do not allow the team to indulge themselves in the stories about how things have been in the past and why they did or did not work. Too much analysis can lead to paralysis. These so-called stories can prevent the team from moving forward by continually dredging up past events.
- Inquiry helps us notice the bridges that can be built between people and various functional areas.
- Inquiry helps us to continue to "check in" with ourselves and each other, to pause, to reflect on each step of the process.

# LEADERSHIP STYLE

Inquiry is an open-ended process. That is, there is no fixed point to attain. It is process-oriented rather than results-oriented. Powerful inquiry allows participants to cut through their filters and beliefs to see things as they really are. Leaders should guide, not direct. They should be Socratic in style – that is, lead with questions, not answers. Be transparent. Be authentic. Eliminate the preconceived notion that you have all the answers or that you understand what is going on, even if you do. Assume nothing. Look for openings. An Action-Learning Team leader needs to be able to tolerate ambiguity and help the team do the same.

# LEADERSHIP CHARACTERISTICS TO EMBRACE

- Question effectively to evoke team thinking and action
- Listen actively for thoughts and feelings
- Summarize the information generated by the team
- Articulate your own thoughts and feelings without undue influence on the team
- Focus the team's attention on the key issues
- Create a high level of trust and respect by and for the team
- Think in terms of "we" instead of "I"
- Have high standards – do not tolerate mediocrity in yourself or others
- Be results-oriented, a catalyst in producing great results
- Ponder and question
- Focus on the process, not the results
- Create and build a sense of contribution
- Eliminate the bureaucratic thinking that clutters the process
- Put the hard truths on the table
- Communicate expectations clearly
- Fail often in order to succeed sooner

- Create a sense of urgency

**Avoid Premature Closure:** Inquiry is an open-ended process. It does not frame a preconceived notion of one person's particular vision. Questions eliminate the possibility of solving the problem too quickly or rushing to a conclusion. If an answer is reached too quickly, it eliminates all other opportunities for a solution.

# TENDENCIES TO AVOID IN THIS PHASE

- Inadequate preparation
- Right people not on the team
- Unclear issue selection
- Sidetracked by personality issues
- Action items vague
- No priorities: too many items to implement
- No follow-up on issues generated
- Truncating the Inquiry process
- Micro-managing the team
- Dictating the outcome
- Team continuing to tell old stories
- Not grounded in reality

# 3 DESIGN - INNOVATING THE ROADMAP FORWARD

## PURPOSE

Where the goal of Inquiry is to dig deep into the root causes of the problem and discover the underlying Potential Improvement Points (PIPs), the purpose of the Design stage is to prioritize those PIPs and then decide where one will get the maximum leverage.

It is the Design stage that will allow the ALT to create a true framework for change. Design is more than just a plan for how to get from here to there; it is a way to create an *innovative* blueprint for solving the PIPs discovered during Inquiry. Tom Kelly (Kelley and Littman 2001, p. 55), co-founder of IDEO, one of the world's most influential industrial design firms, refers to innovation as not just about the myth of the genius working alone waiting for brilliant ideas to strike; it is about the innate capacity for everyone to be creative and how to tap into that creativity in a collaborative and powerful process. This is the road map that will allow the ALT to come up with highly creative and "outside-the-box" solutions.

The goal at the end of Design is to have a clearly defined and specific road map for deploying either a pilot (whenever possible) or the initiative itself. The team develops a strategy for solutions by including key stakeholders – the customers, suppliers and key vendors or anyone else who may be touched by the problem and the solution. While it is not always possible to include these stakeholders in the design, the question should always be posed: Do we need to include anyone else's point of view that may be affected by our design?

Key stakeholders may be both inside and outside the organization. For example, you may want to include key vendors, suppliers, and customers in your design process at certain points, whenever decisions are being made that may have a significant affect on them. There are many access points to the stakeholders in the Design stage. For example, as we will see in the following section, when Boeing was designing its 777 aircraft, they brought their key customers in at specific points in the design process to ensure that the solutions they were creating were "fit for purpose."

## ACTION-LEARNING AND AEROSPACE INDUSTRIAL DESIGN

At one point, Boeing had planned to raise the level of its wing several feet above the height of their current aircraft. Their key customers alerted them to the fact that if Boeing went ahead with this plan, the airlines would have to purchase new fleets of refueling trucks, or hire seven-foot-tall technicians to run them, since none of their current vehicles could reach high enough to refuel the aircraft. Of course, this raised the real cost of ownership for the 777 significantly. By including this critical input from their customers, Boeing sold more aircraft and the airlines that purchased them did not incur significant additional cost of ownership. This was a true win-win situation.

Boeing and its major contractors have learned from these lessons. As we write this, the new Boeing 787 Dream Liner is slated for delivery in 2008, and Teague, a leading-edge industrial design firm, is using Action-Learning Teams to bring a new level of innovation and comfort to the interior of this long-range passenger aircraft. With incredible competitive pressure coming from Airbus, Teague's goal was to demonstrate a superior experience for passengers in a concept jet that was unveiled on a world tour in June of 2005. Rather than organizing along traditional functional lines to accomplish this, we worked with Teague to bring together designers, engineers, factory assembly, vendors, and their client Boeing to create one cohesive Action-Learning Team.

*Figure 4: Interior of the Boeing 777-200LR aircraft showcased at the 2005 Paris Air Show. First class cabin and business class cabin were developed using an Action-Learning Team approach.*

The goal, says Program Manager Wayne Yutani, is to "ensure that all of these functional groups share a common 'strategic intent' and then act in concert to create an unparalleled experience for passengers. No traditional training program could prepare our team for this complex initiative" (LaRue and Ivany 2004; LaRue 2005). Instead, expert facilitation was coupled with Action-Learning to develop the precise capabilities and competencies necessary to create a turnkey solution. This way of working together does not necessarily come naturally to a team of highly specialized knowledge workers, each having a different job to do. But because tactical decisions have strategic consequences, we worked with each individual contributor within the team to learn to see their role in the context of the whole initiative, and to act accordingly.

# OBSERVATION

It is critical that we assume the perspective of our customers when we design our products and services. This is easier said than done, however. For example, Charles Schwab constantly tries to find ways to provide his brand of services in a way that would make him happy *if he were a customer.*

Sometimes, though, it is not enough to simply just ask the customer. At IDEO, a company referred to by Fortune Magazine as "*Innovation U,*" the leaders felt that it was not enough just to ask the end user of their product or service, or even put themselves in their shoes. Tom Kelly (Kelley and Littman 2001) states in his book *The Art of Innovation* that "the same factor prevents you from learning that your meat loaf tastes like sawdust. Your dinner guests are too polite to tell you the unvarnished truth, too wrapped up in trying to give you the expected answer." If you ask and they tell you "fine," there is no information in that statement. In fact, at IDEO, they refer to "fine" as a four-letter word.

One must go beyond just *asking* customers what they want. More than likely, most of them "cannot articulate the *true* answer". As in the case of the meatloaf, "The problem is that your guests may like to eat, but they're not food critics." (p. 28)

It is not your customer's job to become visionary or creative about their needs. Leon Segal, the IDEO human factors expert, states that "Innovation begins with an eye." It requires an observation of how the people who are going to be affected by the initiative operate right now, where they are. It also requires caring about the people who will be affected by your design.

Let's go on the assumption that you've assembled an Action-Learning Team, that you have the right people on the team, and that the team members have identified the core PIP or initiative that they want to focus on. Well-meaning people in your organization will probably tell you they already know what the problem is and that the solution is obvious. They have a preconceived notion of not only the problem, but the solution, which eliminates the opportunity for inspiration and creativity.

Walk around the department or area that is the source of the PIP and observe the day-to-day operations as if you were an outsider. Gareth Morgan (1997, p. 129) equates this process with becoming an organizational anthropologist. Go to the area in the company where the PIPs reside. Look at the people's behavior, the words they use, the beliefs they have and especially the various rituals of their daily routine and observe how they really work. Don't assume that the work is being conducted according to the directions prescribed by management, job descriptions, or the formal organization chart, but rather simply observe how the work is actually being accomplished. What you find may astound you, and this information is the source of true innovative design.

Observation and inspiration should not necessarily have to be formal. Simply notice how people interact regarding the PIP you are trying to solve. Become hyper-aware. Ask questions and listen carefully. If you are designing a solution for an end user or customer, they must be included in the process.

Years ago, Xerox (Lesser, Fontaine et al. 2000) decided to put all their manuals online for the copier techs who were operating in the field. They assumed that this would cut down on costs of printing the manuals and give the techs more immediate access to a larger database. However, no one asked the techs what would be useful to them. When no one had accessed the Web sites, the techs informed management that the online manuals were useless, as the technicians rarely used manuals in the field. They relied on experience and a simple yet highly effective system of word of mouth to solve problems. Those who had created the most effective community of practice (see Chapter 6 of this volume) were the most successful and innovative at their jobs.

Be sure the observation process embraces both the designers of the solutions and those deeply involved in the problem. Observation is organic, since it is not enough to just watch what people do or hear what they say. It is an intuitive, anthropologic discovery of the underlying motivations for why people behave the way they do.

It is quite possible that there are people in the organization who have created "bypass" systems or workarounds for the problems they are experiencing. You can learn much from watching people who break the rules. People who maintain the status quo and follow directions often won't be very innovative. As leaders, we can learn much by simply observing and then integrating these work-around solutions into our design of formal work processes, always allowing for flexibility and innovation in our designs. This is also known as the principle of *emergent design*, which simply states that we must allow ample room for solutions to emerge from the minds of those who are closest to the problem, being careful not to over-prescribe or to define so much in our solutions that we leave no room for adaptive improvisation. Said another way, we have found that it is best to allow results to emerge as a natural outcome of a healthy process.

# BRAINSTORMING

Brainstorming is a process that employs very specific techniques to discover new creative solutions. Kelly (Kelley and Littman 2001) states that:

> Many businesspeople treat brainstorming as a check box, a threshold variable, like 'Can you ride a bicycle?' or 'Do you know how to tie your shoes?' They overlook the possibility that brainstorming can be a skill, an art, more like playing the piano than tying your shoes. You're always learning and can get continuously better. (p. 55)

Prior to beginning a brainstorming process, it is critical to consider whether the right people are participating in this process. While the ALT is responsible for the process, we encourage that the key stakeholders be invited to the session, when appropriate, and particularly if they are customers, key vendors, or suppliers. However, the ALT may already be composed of the right people for brainstorming. Just be sure to check that there is sufficient understanding of the specific nature of the PIP before the session. Since this is not possible in all cases, then the perspective of these additional stakeholders needs to be included as part of the observation.

When deciding who should be at a brainstorming session, consider the following:

- Who will be most affected by this decision?
- Who can provide more information?
- What cross-functional roles should be represented?

Brainstorming is not a typical meeting. It doesn't have to be off-site, nor does it need to take up the entire day. It is a very creative, informal way to discover solutions. People don't take notes in the normal way, nor do they take turns speaking. When done properly, there is a certain amount of energy that becomes difficult to sustain. IDEO limits brainstorming sessions to an hour to an hour and a half maximum. We recommend no more than this.

Tom Kelly (2001, p. 55) asserts that brainstorming should be woven into the "cultural fabric of your organization". It is like a muscle that needs to be developed. If you want to stay in shape, you go to the gym regularly. If you want to create a culture of innovation, Action-Learning Teams need to employ brainstorming as a skill developed over time.

It is important to develop solutions that are continually *emerging and evolving*. It is the essence of what Argyris and Schön (1996) referred to as double loop learning, or the ability of a team or an organization to learn in an ongoing way. This not only challenges the status quo, but the operating norms, assumptions, and the context from within which the problems arise.

Brainstorming expands a group's capacity to become creative. It challenges standard business paradigms and typical solutions, allowing innovation to emerge. There are specific ways to create an effective brainstorming session:

# BE FOCUSED

Become crystal clear about what the design is intended to solve. Define the PIP that you are attempting to solve and be sure that it is articulated specifically, externally focused on the customer, rather than internally focused on organizational goals or processes. Review the PIP and ask what you need as a team to make this process successful.

- What are the must haves? Money? Authority? Whose influence do you need to court?
- What are the nice to haves? It may be nice to have more money, for example, but not a necessity. What did you think was so important, that you might be able to do without?

- What are the better not haves? Perhaps there are certain things or people that would be obstacles to the initiative.

Becoming clear involves the group letting go and attaining what Zen practitioners call "beginner's mind." Steve Hagan (Hagen 1999, p. 87) states that we "tend to form our minds in rigid forms of will. We unwittingly follow hidden assumed rules which manifest in hidden patterns of thought and behavior." Setting the conditions for brainstorming breaks those patterns to permit innovative and atypical ideas to occur.

Since the brainstorming session is short and time is valuable, it is not always necessary to do anything special to warm up the group unless:

- The group has not worked together before
- Most of the group does not brainstorm frequently
- The group seems distracted by pressing but unrelated issues (Kelley and Littman 2001, p. 60).

## KEEP IT LIGHT

IDEO encourages the use of playful rules. Their idea is to create an atmosphere of fun without debate or criticism, which can drain the energy of the session very quickly. IDEO uses such rules as "be visual," "go for quantity," and "encourage wild ideas." We also like "no stories," "solutions, not more problems," and "fail often in order to succeed sooner."

Accumulate as many ideas as possible. Linus Pauling stated that the best way to get good ideas is to get a lot of ideas. Do not edit, judge, debate or analyze. Go for the quantity. At this time, nothing is off the table. Use game-playing and role-playing. Use as much physicality as possible. In our consulting practice, we like to use multiple flip charts. We post them around the room and split the session into three to five teams of five to eight people each. Each team gets a pad and various colored markers. Sometimes we have used paper tablecloths to encourage participants to write, draw or use symbols to express themselves.

## USE SPATIAL MEMORY

Encourage writing the flow of ideas down on something that is visible to the whole group. Our consulting group had a brainstorming session as part of a workshop with 100 people in Leon, Mexico. We had large pads posted with masking tape all around the room. We accumulated ideas and the participants drew pictures, mind maps, diagrams and expressions. Each time a paper was filled, it was posted on the wall. Forty-five minutes later, when we were done, the wall was covered with multicolored drawings, words and diagrams. To refer to a particular idea, participants went to the place on the wall where they had created it and, in the process, remembered the mind-set they had during the creation process. The act of getting up and walking over to a particular point brought back the thought process they had while creating the idea.

## GET PHYSICAL

Brainstorming is a visual process. It is expressed through the sketches and words of the participants, but it is also carried out by members attempting to get their point across by role-playing or mimicking behavior patterns to see how they might be changed.

Brainstorming should be a fun, energizing experience that does not feel like a regular meeting. It should take idea creation and solving of PIPs to the next level. Although the process should be engaged in lightly, it should be taken seriously, as great brainstorming can create powerful new ways of thinking.

# CREATE

When the brainstorming process is complete, there may be one or more ideas for a design of an initiative that the group may want to pursue. This is the time to go from quantity to quality. The goal of the group as a whole (or in two or three smaller groups) is to focus the knowledge gained from the brainstorming to create innovative solutions.

As the design takes shape and the group members develop possible solutions, then we ask:

- **Is it easy to use?** The solution cannot be so complicated that the stakeholders either don't understand it, or simply won't use it.
- **Is it aligned with the company's strategy?** Any good solution needs to be aligned with the company's strategy or it risks being shot down by senior management.
- **Are there sufficient resources to execute the solution?** Any initiative without sufficient manpower, money, or time will die on the vine.

# PILOT WHEN POSSIBLE

Whenever possible, pilot, simulate, or prototype the design. Creating a pilot allows the group to test the initiative and mitigate the challenges, while learning from them. It is the answer to the question, "Who does this impact and how is this going to affect them?"

This is the essence of reflection in action. Deploy the pilot, assess what works and what needs improvement, and adjust accordingly. Trying out the potential solution on a limited scale allows the ALT to discover the problems that are bound to occur and determine how the deployment will impact the stakeholders. Evaluate the pilot and determine if it will achieve the results desired, before deploying it company-wide.

In some cases, an initiative cannot be piloted. Perhaps it involves a restructuring of an entire department and would engage too many people. It is still critical in these cases to be sure the ALT understands how their design will impact the stakeholders. Get the stakeholders involved at different points in the initial stages of deployment. Continually monitor what is working and what could be improved.

Ask:

- What was our intended outcome?
- What was the actual outcome?
- What are three behaviors we want to eliminate?
- What are three behaviors we want to sustain?

## KEY QUESTIONS TO EXPLORE IN THIS PHASE

- What is the scale of this initiative?
- How much engagement from the organization will it require?
- What are the obstacles?
- What are the workarounds?
- What is the path of least resistance, enabling us to move more quickly?
- What is the final desired outcome?
- Who and what will be affected by this solution?
- How will we identify and measure success when we're done?
- What types of people are needed?

  **Drivers and Producers** – People who are results-oriented, task-driven, and effective. People who are driven by making something happen. They are creating results.

**Entrepreneurs and Visionaries** – People who are proactive and think about the future. They focus on *why* an initiative is necessary.

**Analysts and Administrative** – People who think about systems and procedures. They pay attention to detail. They focus on *how* things get done.

**Consensus Builders** – People who are good at integrating teams. They covet consensus and teamwork. They focus on *who* gets it done.

# TENDENCIES TO AVOID IN THIS PHASE

- Creating a design that fixes the symptoms rather than the underlying problem
- Allowing individuals to control the design or come up with their own design outside the team
- Creating a design that doesn't address the issue
- Deploying the design prematurely without deploying a pilot (whenever possible)
- Not including customer and key vendor feedback in a design
- Ignoring institutionalized dysfunctional patterns of behavior.
- The design must consider workarounds and any structure problems that could impede deployment of the initiative

# LEADERSHIP STYLE

The leadership style at this phase should be facilitative. The leader must help the team create unique solutions. The goal is to educate, coach, and advise, while allowing a solution to *emerge*. A key component is to keep the team moving forward, while allowing them to cultivate ideas and think creatively.

Look for links between points that can build the framework for a constructive solution. Keep the team together. Discourage individuals from taking the ball and running with it independently or prematurely.

## CHARACTERISTICS TO EMBRACE

- Ability to embrace ambiguity
- Ability to keep the team focused
- Ability to inject ideas that contribute to the process without taking over the initiative
- Ability to keep the team moving through confusion, doubt, ambiguity, and uncertainty

## CHARACTERISTICS TO AVOID

- Directive leadership
- Creating new problems to solve
- Poor direction or instruction
- Lack of preparation and due diligence
- Allowing "the boss" to set the agenda
- Too much structure during brainstorming

# 4 DEPLOYMENT - TRANSFORMATION IN ACTION

## PURPOSE

The purpose of deployment is to implement initiatives in the workplace while continuing to identify and exploit unforeseen opportunities. Our goal is also to break the barriers that impede our progress in the initiation of change. It is to deploy Action-Learning Teams that are cross-functional, systemically focused, and highly collaborative in their approach.

In this phase, participants will discover how to implement initiatives with power and influence by building bridges of common interest. When accomplished correctly, deployment will accelerate the discovery process by addressing how to break down any barriers the team is experiencing that are preventing them from implementing these initiatives.

Deployment involves the continuing assessment in action of what is going well and what is not. The most seasoned strategy is only as good as its execution. Designs that seem full of promise on the white board can rapidly fall apart in day-to-day implementation. The goal of the Deployment Phase is to make the change initiatives designed in the previous phase a reality by continuing to reflect, take action, and adjust course in order to move the organization toward its desired end-state.

# THE PROCESS

Quite often, deployment of an initiative is done in an ad hoc way, even though great thought has gone into the design of the initiative. The reason is that any time organizations undergo change, there will be resistance.

When employees are faced with novelty, change, or perceived threat – work teams, organizational departments, even entire companies often react with defensiveness and unhealthy forms of controlling behavior.

Gareth Morgan (1997, p. 259) states that organizations tend to have a "fixed notion of who they are or what they can be and are determined to impose or sustain that identity at all costs". The tendency in times of change is for teams, individuals and organizations to hold on to the fixed identity or vision they have for themselves. When change is introduced into the mixture, there is a natural resistance, since even healthy initiatives aimed at improving operational performance are often perceived as threats to the status quo and to formal position, rank, and hierarchy.

Organizational culture is composed of structures created by the people within the organization for dealing with anxiety and uncertainty. When change is introduced, it challenges those norms and the fixed identity the organization holds for itself. In order to assist in breaking some of these barriers:

- Pay attention to the current state of the organization. People may learn what they need to do, but the inherent systems and culture may put up resistance.
- Pay attention to the norms of the groups and the surrounding culture in which they work every day.
- Find the best place to put your crowbar. Drive the change from the right place in the organization. Whenever possible, start at the top.

- Develop a language for the change initiative. Daniel Goleman (Goleman, Boyatzis et al. 2002, p. 233) refers to this as "meaningful words that capture the spirit…by symbolizing ideas, ideals and emotionally intelligent leadership practices."

Peter Drucker (1999, p. 73) states that "you cannot manage change, you can only be ahead of it." Drucker goes on to state that it is up to an organization to lead change. People accept that change is unavoidable, but this is the equivalent of accepting the inevitable instead of leading the way. There tends to be an inherent resistance to change and it should be expected throughout the organization.

# COMMUNICATION

It is critical in the deployment stage to gain as much of a shared vision with the organization as possible. According to Morgan (1997, p. 147), "It is the ability to create the appropriate systems of shared meaning that can mobilize the efforts of people in pursuit of desired aims and objectives."

Those that are affected by the change effort need to have a common understanding of the goals and direction of the organization. The greater the common view of the future, the better the possibility of coordinated actions that create successful change efforts. This is where many leaders miscalculate the importance of communication; they will under-communicate or send inconsistent messages. The result is a stalled change effort.

Even when there is a significant effort to communicate a new vision of the future, having that vision accepted in the hearts and minds of the employees takes time. People's first reaction to change is to ask a lot of questions. How does this affect me? How does this affect my department? How is the organization going to change? Is there another way to do this? Am I going to be able to do what is expected with these changes? Is this for real, or will it eventually go away?

The ALT should be aware of the need to communicate effectively. Members representing various areas of the organization should be communicating with their people along the way and receiving their input. It is good to involve a PR or corporate communications person early in the change process to start crafting a communication plan.

John Kotter (1996, p. 90) describes in his book *Leading Change* seven key elements in the effective communication of vision that continue to hold true:

1.  **Simplicity:** All jargon and techno-babble must be eliminated. ALTs need to create a language for change: simple, with emotional impact that everyone can understand.
2.  **Metaphor, analogy, and example:** An image is worth a thousand words. There are hundreds of messages every day competing for people's attention. Become imaginative in using words and images.
3.  **Multiple forums:** Big meetings and small, memos and newsletters, formal and informal interaction – all are effective for spreading the word. Use as many different vehicles as possible for communication. When the same message comes from multiple directions, it stands a better chance of being retained.
4.  **Repetition:** Ideas sink in deeply only after they have been heard many times.
5.  **Leadership by example:** Behavior from important people that is inconsistent with the vision overwhelms other forms of communication.
6.  **Explanation of seeming inconsistencies:** Unaddressed inconsistencies undermine the credibility of all communication.
7.  **Give and take:** Two-way communication is always more powerful than one-way communication.

# RESISTANCE TO CHANGE

Deploying change in an organization challenges the fixed identities that teams, workgroups or entire organizations have established for themselves. While not every initiative will encounter resistance, it is a common occurrence whenever major change is introduced in organizations. It is important to note the potential forms resistance can take. While this is not an exhaustive list, Action-Learning Teams should be aware of the various forms of resistance that may be manifested along the way.

Deploying a major change initiative is an innovative act. It is the attempt to bring unique solutions to an environment that tends to covet certainty and resist change. Here are some forms of resistance that can occur:

- **Complacency**: Kotter (1996) describes complacency in over-managed and over-led cultures by people who are taught that certain actions are not sensible. This arises particularly in highly-controlled environments. Complacency is a move toward risk aversion and away from ambiguity. To many in an organization, complacency is a way to respond to change and maintain the status quo.

- **Drama**: Sometimes entire departments and organizations can participate in a culture of self-dramatization. Shared stories sometimes take on lives of their own and distract from the task at hand. People personalize certain issues and look for intent behind every action.

- **Victim Mentality**: Employees and even entire departments can act like victims based on the perceived effect of management or other departments. Management can play the victim role by blaming their frustrations on the employees or the change initiative itself. Playing victim to a certain condition (e.g., "if only management would change") lends significance to one's identity and maintains the fixed notion of powerlessness. A team, individual or organization acting as a victim holds others to the prospect of further dysfunctional behavior. It is the antithesis of change and does more to keep people from being responsible for their situation than anything else.

# TAKING ACTION

In deployment, an ALT and the leadership need to be aware of the following steps to inculcate the initiatives with power and effectiveness:

- **Create a sense of urgency.** To mobilize the energy of the organization toward change, there needs to be a sense of urgency created by communicating honestly about the problems and opportunities facing the organization and the rewards for capitalizing on these. It is important to identify and minimize the sources of complacency.
- **Reduce traditional thinking.** Work "outside the box." Become innovative in getting people to accept new ideas.
- **Focus on the process, not the results.** Allow the results to emerge as a natural outcome of a healthy process. Also known as *emergent* design, this principle states that prematurely focusing on the end result may not give enough time for buy-in of the initiative being deployed.
- **Expect and tolerate ambiguity, setbacks and messiness of the process**. Tolerance of ambiguity is a key attribute of being an effective agent of change. This is because ambiguity, or that in-between state, is a natural phase in the process of change. It is like being "between the trapezes" – letting go of one position and heading for another. It is uncomfortable and there is a tendency to want to go back to our last known position.
- **Create small wins**. "Kaizen" is described by the Japanese as making small, incremental improvements over time. It is gradual, ongoing and never-ending. John Kotter (1996, p. 121-122) suggests that small wins have three characteristics:

- o They are visible. Large numbers of people can see for themselves whether the result is real or hype.
- o They are unambiguous. There is little argument over the call.
- o They are clearly related to the change effort.
- **Encourage reflection.** The cultivation of the practice to reflect *in action* is important. Ask appropriate questions:
  - o What is working?
  - o What could be immediately improved?
- **Look for common interests.** People execute and implement when they have common interests. While management is concerned with the interests of the shareholders, for example, and the workers are concerned with their security and benefits, they can create common interests by considering the end user of the product or service. By working together to give the customer a superior experience, both parties achieve their objectives.
- **Come from service.** Act in a way that recognizes and addresses the needs and benefits of others.
- **Don't try to be perfect.** Take immediate action, even if you only attain 50 percent of your goal.
- **If you make a mistake, address it immediately.** Use the After Action Review (AAR) process (see Chapter 11) to not only correct any missteps but facilitate organizational learning.

In a recent article from the *McKinsey Quarterly* on "The Psychology of Change Management" (McKinsey and Company., 2003), Emily Lawson and Colin Price stated that:

Employees will alter their mind sets only if they see the point of the change and agree with it – at least enough to give it a try. The surrounding structures (reward and recognition systems, for example) must be in tune with the new behavior. Employees must have the skills to do what is required. Finally, they must see people they respect actively modeling the behaviors. Each of these conditions is realized independently; together they add up to a way of changing the behavior of people in organizations by changing attitudes about what can and should happen at work.

In addition, the change process needs to take on a life of its own. The only way this can happen is to establish a critical mass throughout the organization with the people who own the change and are responsible for it. And it is not just a critical mass of knowledge and understanding on an analytical level, it must be within the heart and soul of the people in the organization. People cannot institute this type of change by edict and make it sustainable.

# THE PHASES OF DEPLOYMENT

Teams can go through certain phases throughout the deployment of their initiatives. These phases apply both to the ALT itself and to the organization as a whole. This is not a fixed or structured notion that everyone will encounter; however, it is critical to be *aware* of the stages so that the members of the ALT or the leadership of the company can identify the obstacles and address them appropriately.

# INDUCTION

Induction is primarily a time at the beginning stages of deployment when the ALT and the executive team are most optimistic about the potential to achieve a given result. It can be a time of hope and anticipation. After completion of the design stage, expectations of the ALT can run high. There is optimism about the future. Teams begin to create a common sense of purpose as they embark on the new initiatives. Lofty goals are often set since they are created from the wellspring of the team's imagination. There are few constraints and limitless possibilities.

# DISILLUSIONMENT

It is at this point that the gap between what is imagined and the ALTs ability to execute can become apparent. While Induction is future-focused, Disillusionment, to the degree it may occur, is set squarely in the present, complete with time and budgetary pressures and the need to create tangible results. Carefully conceived plans often times don't work according to expectations, leading to the rise of doubts and insecurities about the initiative, the team or the strategy.

John Kotter (1996, p 4) states that "Personnel problems often lurking beneath the surface of a team – all too easily ignored during placid times – come to the fore during times of change." In fact, any previously suppressed behavior or dysfunctional pattern of process, structure, vision, value or people will be stirred up during this time of change.

Group members may start questioning themselves. They may begin to doubt their own or others' ability to generate results. People revert under pressure to their "backup" behaviors, traits they would exhibit if backed into a corner. They can begin to attack others, become submissive, or withdraw into passivity.

The best-laid plans of any change initiative can be in danger of becoming stalled because of the team's discouragement about the realities of the challenge. Hope can quickly become despair. Disillusionment can lead to organizational malaise, abandonment of the initiative, or ineffective execution.

While every team has the potential to go through this period of disillusionment, the key is for teams to be informed that disillusionment is a natural phase and it is important that the team work through it. To move quickly through Disillusionment, leaders need to help teams become conscious of the symptoms of this phase and the fact that this is a temporary condition.

The key is to continue to concentrate on the *specific* operational, behavioral and organizational gaps they are targeting. Only then can the team complete their initiatives to produce a change going deep into the culture of the company.

# BREAKTHROUGH

On the surface, Breakthrough can appear similar to Induction and, if you aren't paying attention, you might miss the subtle differences. There is still a sense of hope and optimism in Breakthrough, but this phase is a milestone, a particular turning point in the initiative. There is an atmosphere of mutual respect that didn't exist before. People are increasingly conscientious as they listen to each other while the breakthrough process occurs. There are small, continual adjustments being made to the initiative and a belief that things may be getting better. Problems are being resolved more quickly. There may be conflict, but now it's more constructive and less destructive.

However, the fundamental difference between Breakthrough and Induction is that the team has already been *through* Disillusionment. Having experienced the highs of Induction and the lows of Disillusionment, participants know that the future holds something in between. There is a subtle but powerful difference in the way problems are approached and conflict is addressed.

It was once said that flirtation is *intention* without *attention*. Breakthrough is the same. It's a flirtation with the *possibility* of profound change. It is the ability to produce results through *focused intention* without attention. New skill sets are being learned and, even though it may seem awkward at this stage, performance gets easier with practice.

When a child first learns to ride a bike, considerable attention is paid to the mechanics of balance, speed and control. The *intention* to get somewhere is superseded by the *attention* needed to keep riding without falling down. Suddenly the child "gets it," and is riding without help. This begins the process of losing the attention of the mechanics and focusing on the intention of going somewhere.

So it is with Breakthrough. It is the stage when the team and the organization "get it" and begin the process of leaving behind the baggage of Disillusionment.

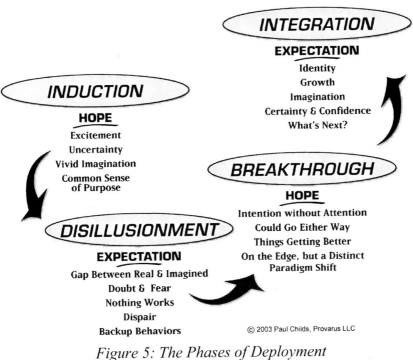

*Figure 5: The Phases of Deployment*

# INTEGRATION

At this point, ALT leaders should focus on consolidating lessons learned from the initiative into replicable processes for future initiatives. What worked well and what can be improved? What are the key lessons the team has learned from the initiative and what are the implications for "business as usual" as well as future initiatives of this kind? It is easy to overlook this phase in the Deployment Cycle and simply move on to other things. Powerful forces of inertia based on previous organizational patterns and power structures can also undermine many change efforts, often in spite of impressive early accomplishments. For these reasons, it is critical to use this opportunity to develop valuable "institutional memory" so that you don't find yourself re-inventing the wheel and repeating potentially costly mistakes in the future. We will focus on this critical phase of the ALT process in the next chapter.

# KEY QUESTIONS TO EXPLORE IN THIS PHASE

- What barriers are standing between where you are and where you want to go? How exactly do you plan to remove them?
- How do you create an increased capacity to initiate effective and lasting change in your organization?
- How do you engage the critical stakeholders in the organization in the deployment of this new strategy?
- How do you create a *culture of influence,* where the new ways of thinking and creating become part of the fabric of organizational life?
- What is your predominant leadership style and how will you use the appropriate leadership styles at each phase of the Deployment Cycle?
- How can you help your team deal with uncertainty and ambiguity?

- What role do tacit and explicit knowledge play in your organization today?

# TENDENCIES TO AVOID IN THIS PHASE

**Discouraging constructive conflict.** Sometimes the problem is not so much the individuals on the team, but how they act once they come together. There are many examples of this in recent corporate scandals. Quite often, CEOs of large organizations come together as part of a board of directors for another company. Instead of encouraging constructive conflict, they continually discourage debate and disagreement. They turn into a team that ultimately values consensus and unity over truth and healthy debate. The team comes to believe that the collective brainpower of the group supplants the need for debate. They become infallible, but also untested. During the Enron debacle, for example, nearly every board vote was unanimous.

**Letting information fit your conclusions.** Conclusions should be drawn from new information and appropriate research that does not fit previously defined constructs. Care should be taken to seek external information and not rely too much on self-generated information.

# LEADERSHIP STYLE

Leadership style needs to be *adaptive* and *flexible* as the team experiences transformation while the initiatives begin to take hold. Conflicts may arise in the team that are not easily resolved. There is a tendency at times to question the team, the team leader, the process of implementation chosen, or the initiative itself. Without proper facilitation, after a period of time the team begins to break down. Communication becomes constrained and ineffective. Blame and finger-pointing prevail. At this point, the group may seek a scapegoat upon which to heap their anxieties and fear of failure.

Leaders are especially vulnerable at this stage as the group seeks to blame those with greater visibility and responsibility. The noted group theorist Wilfred Bion (Bion 1961) termed this stage of development "fight/flight" and described it as a classic group response to uncertainty and ambiguity leading ultimately to persistent task avoidance.

# CREATE A SAFE SPACE; ACCEPT AMBIGUITY

Leaders at this stage must focus on creating a safe space within which team members can learn to tolerate ambiguity and uncertainty while helping them to refocus their attention and energy on the task at hand. The leader also should inform the team ahead of time that this phase of uncertainty will occur and let them know what they might experience. This tends to lessen the impact of this phase.

# CHARACTERISTICS TO EMBRACE

- Encourage constructive conflict
- Become a microcosm for the change you wish to see in your organization
- Tolerate and leverage ambiguity to drive innovation
- Continually educate the team about what they and the organization might experience as they move through the deployment stage
- Encourage reflection in action. Reflect on three behaviors that you want to change and three behaviors that you want to keep, and focus on them consistently.

## Table 1: The Phases of Deployment

# PHASES OF DEPLOYMENT

|  | INDUCTION | DISILLUSIONMENT | BREAKTHROUGH | INTEGRATION |
|---|---|---|---|---|
| **Leadership Style Needed** | Coach | Direct | Consult | Delegate |
| **Time Focus** | Future | Present | Present and Future | Timeless |
| **State** | Temporary Pleasure | Temporary Pain | Intention without Attention | "I am or We are" (Becomes the level of identity) |
| **Stage** | Unconsciously Incompetent | Consciously Incompetent | Consciously Competent | Unconsciously Competent |
| **Individual Manifestation** | I'm excited | I can't do this. This is too hard. | I think I can do this now | This is effortless |
| **Team Manifestation** | We're great together | Internal conflicts, Turf wars | Finally getting results despite differences | Become conscious "thought teams"; knowledge workers |
| **Organization Manifestation** | New Initiative | No Support; No market; Difficulty in execution | Market "cooperates"; Sales | Change in core values; Identity; Becomes market leader |
| **Decision Making** | Long Term | Short Term | Short Term | Long Term |
| **Where It Shows Up** | Heart | Mind | Body | Spirit |

# 5 INTEGRATION - ALIGNING CORE SYSTEMS

## PURPOSE

Change often takes a long time to become part of the organization's DNA, especially in large companies. A number of forces can halt the progress of a change effort before it hits the finish line: turnover of key change agents, distraction of the leadership to other priorities, exhaustion. Short-term wins are key in keeping the momentum going, but the challenge is to not lose the urgency too early. The forces of tradition can take hold with amazing force and speed. The purpose of this section is to look at ways to ensure the change initiative that has been deployed becomes a part of the fabric of the organization. Integration is allowing the change initiative to become part of an organization's DNA.

## HOW TO PERFORM A SUCCESSFUL INTEGRATION

Making a lasting change is not easy because irrational and political resistance doesn't dissipate readily. You may experience success in the early stages of a transformation, but there will be a number of cynical managers and employees that will bide their time and look for opportunities to sabotage the effort at some point along the line. Until change efforts have been embedded in the culture of the organization, they can be very fragile. Many months or years of work can be undone with amazing speed. The key point is that if you let up before the job is done, momentum can be lost and regression may follow.

The areas to focus on to make sure there is alignment with the change effort are:

- Commitment of leadership
- Human Resource Systems
- Training
- Troublesome managers
- Organization structure
- Culture

# COMMITMENT OF LEADERSHIP

Without strong and capable leadership from many people in the organization, major changes don't happen well or at all. The leadership usually embraces the change effort and believes in the value of the transformation or they wouldn't have invested in it in the first place. However, while the change efforts may be successful for a while, they may fail in the long run if leadership doesn't stay committed over time, recognizing there will be inevitable bumps along the way. Since leadership is key to any major change effort, it is essential that the ALT keep the leadership apprised of the successes and challenges along the way. Key leaders may need to be coached on how they need to continue to communicate and reinforce the new vision of the change effort over time.

# HUMAN RESOURCES SYSTEMS

Many change efforts have died a slow death because the HR systems did not align with the new vision or change effort (Kotter 1996; Drucker 1999; Drucker 2002). While you might get results in the short term, if you don't address the built-in incentives and processes that may be at odds with the new vision, the change efforts will eventually be undermined by the reward systems in place. The ALT should enlist a senior HR person as part of the team or include their input soon in the change process.

HR systems that need to be aligned with the new vision or change effort are:

- **Performance Evaluation Processes** – These processes need to reflect the behaviors and results and ensure that they align with the change efforts. This is one important way to reinforce the reality of the changes.
- **Compensation decisions** have to be aligned with the new behaviors or results. If employees hear about the importance of the new changes but get rewarded financially for other results, one can guess what happens to the change efforts.
- **Promotion decisions** need to be aligned and communicated to the organization so that employees see that those who embrace the changes are rewarded with opportunities for advancement.
- **Recruiting and hiring decisions** must reflect the skills and characteristics that support the change efforts.

# TRAINING

Many change efforts require managers and employees to change habits and behaviors that they have had for years. Often when training is provided, it is not the right kind or the timing is wrong. Sometimes people are taught the technical skills of a change effort, but not the social skills or attitudes needed to make the changes work in their areas. Most people will need follow-up to help with problems they may encounter while trying to implement the new changes.

One of the mistakes companies often make is that they don't assess thoroughly enough the new behavior, skills, and attitudes that will be needed when major changes are initiated. Therefore, the amount and kind of training needed to help people make the necessary changes are underestimated. Sometimes it can be the cost of training that gets in the way. However, if the right training is not provided, it can slow down or frustrate the implementation of the change efforts. The ALT needs to be aware of the impact of the change effort on the behaviors, skills, and attitudes of managers and employees and go over that information with the HR or training department as well as the leadership of the organization.

# RELUCTANT MANAGERS

There always seem to be a few key managers who just don't get the new vision or embrace the change efforts. They will undercut the initiatives and create an atmosphere that is counterproductive to the change effort. A bad boss can have a very negative impact on people understanding and embracing the change effort. The issue for some managers is that they don't agree with the changes, their management style is counter to the new changes, or they feel threatened by the change. The number of these troublesome managers and the size of the groups they have responsibility for will determine the negative impact they will have on the overall change initiative, sometimes to the point of stalling or stopping the effort.

There are no easy answers to these problem managers. Often leaders will talk with them, but still be unwilling to demote or fire them when necessary. This is because of political reasons, they are friends, or they don't want to go to that extreme.

A better solution is for leadership to have an honest dialogue with these managers. The leader needs to make clear the vision and his or her expectations of that manager including the time frame in which the changes are expected to occur. The leader should ask how they can help them accomplish this, but be clear that this is the expectation for which the manager will be responsible.

The leader is basically redefining success for the manager in this new initiative. It will become clear whether this manager wants to make it work or not. If not, their removal or demotion becomes more apparent and hopefully less contentious. This approach is fair and objective and has a better chance of coming to an appropriate resolution. It also gives a clear message to the rest of the organization about the commitment of leadership to the change initiative.

# WHY LIVING THE VALUES MATTERS

A major high-tech company was initiating a significant change effort that included revising the direction of the company and their operating philosophy. As part of the change effort, the new mission statement and guiding principles were communicated throughout the organization. The regional president, ironically in charge of the highest-producing region in the company, was not embracing the new direction. More importantly, he was not demonstrating the values and guiding principles that were being communicated to the whole organization. The behavior of this executive was naturally having an adverse impact on that particular region adopting the change.

The CEO had many conversations with this particular regional president about his expectations, but little change was forthcoming. The CEO, who was very committed to the change initiative, finally terminated this otherwise high-performing president and communicated to the company that this person's values and those of the company were not aligned and that he would be better off finding a company that would be a better match with his values.

The impact was huge. The organization began taking this initiative very seriously. They knew where the CEO stood on this change initiative, and it was not just talk. After this incident, the entire company quickly embraced the changes, and the change initiative eventually became part of the core culture of the organization. This change initiative, together with the shift in the core values of the organization, made a significant impact on the success of this company. The CEO said later that, "Sometimes you have to shoot a colonel to get the army in line." While we are not advocating getting rid of someone just for effect, it is best to deal with problem managers, even terminating him or her if necessary, for the sake of the rest of the organization.

# ALIGNING ORGANIZATIONAL STRUCTURE

Structure is not always an obstacle to a major change effort, especially in the early stages, but can undermine the initiative if the structure blocks employees' efforts to implement the new changes. If, for example, the change initiative includes becoming more "customer focused," the organizational structure may need to be modified to accommodate these changes. The frontline employees may take on more responsibility, but may bump up against a structure with too many levels and too much decision-making authority vested in the middle. As the employees try to implement the new vision, they are second-guessed by middle management. After a period of time, the frontline people will become discouraged and revert back to their old ways of operating.

If structural issues are not addressed in a timely manner then the risk is that the employees will become frustrated and the transformational effort will fail. Even if you later try to change some of the structural issues, you have lost energy needed to make the change effort a reality. The ALT should look at the structure in how it helps or hinders the change effort and recommend initial changes.

# CULTURE

John Kotter (1996) defines *Culture* as the norms of behavior and shared values among a group of people (p.148). Again, we have defined culture as these norms that are brought into the company from the outside and are the result of the individuals' past experience and beliefs. If the people with these attitudes were to leave the company, the culture would change.

These norms of behavior are common or pervasive ways of acting in a group; those who fit in are rewarded and those who do not are punished. Shared values are goals and attitudes that tend to shape group behavior and persist over time even when group membership changes.

There can be culture elements that effect the whole organization, so-called corporate culture, and there can be culture elements that are specific to a division or function (i.e., Engineering, New York region). Culture is important because it can influence human behavior, can be difficult to change, and because it is almost invisible it is hard to directly address.

When the new approaches of the change effort don't align with the various cultures of the organization, they will be at risk of not being fully adopted. The new practices have not been strongly tied to the group norms and values.

As John Kotter (1996; 1999; Kotter and Cohen 2002) suggests, culture is powerful for three primary reasons:

1. Because individuals are selected and indoctrinated so well.

2. Because the culture exerts itself through the actions of hundreds or thousands of people.
3. Because all of this happens without much conscious intent and thus is difficult to challenge or even discuss.

Because organizational culture has this kind of influence, the new approaches generated by a major change effort must somehow be tied firmly to culture or the change effort can become fragile and eventually flounder.

Many times the core culture is not at odds with the new vision. However, some specific norms or practices may be. "The challenge is to graft the new practices onto the old roots while killing off the inconsistent pieces" (1999, p. 151). It is difficult to attempt to tie new approaches to a culture that is compatible, but when there are significant inconsistencies between the two cultures, the challenge is even greater.

Culture changes only after the people change their behavior, experience positive results, and see the benefits over time. They also must see the connection between the new practices and the overall improvement in the organization. Attitude and behavior change first, then the new practices show results, and toward the end of the change cycle the new approaches become integrated into the culture.

While the impact to the culture happens in the last stages of change, the Action-Learning Team needs to be sensitive to the cultural issues in the first stages of the change process. This is why we suggest that the ALT assess in the Inquiry stage what is really rewarded and punished in the organization. This provides a sense of what the culture is and how certain behaviors or results are being discouraged or reinforced. It is important to be aware of how much the existing culture needs to be changed to accommodate the application of the change initiative.

Kotter (1996) suggests the following on how to anchor change in a culture:

- **Comes last, not first:** Most alterations in norms and shared values come at the end of the transformation process.
- **Depends on results:** New approaches usually sink into a culture only after it is very clear that they work and are superior to old methods.
- **Requires a lot of talk:** Without verbal instruction and support, people are often reluctant to admit the validity of new practices.
- **May involve turnover:** Sometimes the only way to change a culture is to change key people.
- **Makes decisions on succession crucial:** If promotion processes are not changed to be compatible with the new practices, the old culture will reassert itself.

# LEADERSHIP CHARACTERISTICS IMPORTANT AT THIS PHASE

Most ALTs are not still meeting during the latter part of the Integration phase. However, the team members should continue to influence their areas as well as the leadership to ensure the proper integration of the change initiative. The ALT leader needs to shift his or her focus to coaching the company leadership, team members, HR, training, etc. in order to maintain the focus on the long-term integration of the behaviors, skills, and attitudes of the change initiative.

# THINGS TO AVOID IN THIS PHASE

The following is a list of things to avoid to be sure the transition is properly integrated in an organization:

- **Under-communicating** – most companies vastly underestimate the amount and quality of communication needed to get the employees willing to help make the change initiative a reality. They think a few meetings, a few memos, and newsletter articles are enough. Effective communication is both in words and action, with the latter being more influential. All it takes to undermine or kill a business transition is for the actions of key leaders to be inconsistent with the words they speak.

- **Underestimating the time and effort to fully integrate the initiative** – Many times organizations celebrate victory after the first sign of success of the initiative. While it is great to recognize short-term successes, it is a mistake to think that the effort is over. The changes need to become part of the fabric of the organization and a transparent part of the culture. This takes time, in many cases years, depending on the size of the change. There has to be a commitment to ride the pony to the finish line.

- **Not keeping the focus and energy needed to reinforce the behaviors and attitudes** – There needs to be a high degree of urgency in the organization to be successful at a major change effort. Many times the energy is there in the beginning, but after a period of time complacency sets in and the energy and focus necessary to sustain the change effort wanes.

Aligning structure, core processes, and values with the new direction of the company are essential to creating sustainable change. The process of integration is thus a critical aspect of any change initiative. While this is the final phase in the change process, the principles of integration must be carefully considered and woven into the change initiative early in the process.

# PART II

# ACTION-LEARNING TEAMS: AN ESSENTIAL COMPONENT OF ORGANIZATIONAL STRATEGY

In this section, we will explore the concept of Action-Learning Teams and why we believe that they are becoming an essential component of organizational strategy. We will show you how to identify where Action-Learning Teams may already be operating in your organization and how you, as a leader, can work with these teams to become wellsprings of innovation in your organization. We will examine a number of examples of Action-Learning Teams and how they helped organizations cope with an increasing pace of change, technological complexity, and heightened competition with a focus on creating a superior end-customer experience.

# 6 HOW CAN ACTION-LEARNING TEAMS BENEFIT YOUR ORGANIZATION?

## ACTION-LEARNING TEAMS AND THE INFORMAL ORGANIZATION

If you learn to look the right way, you will see that something akin to Action-Learning Teams already operates within your organization. Resembling "communities of practice" (CoP) (Lave and Wenger 1991; Allee 1997; Wenger 1998; Brown and Duguid 2000; 2002; Wenger, McDermott et al. 2002; Allee 2003), these groups comprise the informal organization that has learned how to work around barriers imposed by the traditional organizational structure, hierarchy, and procedures to get the job done.

The problem is that these groups, by their nature, often have to work under the radar, and sometimes even pose a threat to those who derive their legitimacy through formal rank and hierarchy. As such, communities of practice are generally not formally sanctioned and therefore tend to be ad hoc, underutilized, and under-resourced. It follows that these informal groups are going to be far less strategic in focus.

For example, Rich, a senior manager of the wireless data division of a national wireless telecom company, said that it was as if he could look at his organization under two different kinds of light and see two very different patterns of activity. Under normal light, Rich saw his team of several hundred highly skilled engineers and technicians working within a carefully defined organizational chart indicating a complex series of reporting relationships and authority structures. Within each functional area were jobs with responsibilities that were spelled out in detail and formally sanctioned by the human resources department.

After working with us, Rich said that it was as if he turned off these lights and turned on a black light. What he saw under the black light fundamentally changed the way he thought about and *hence how he managed* his team. He saw under the black light how work actually got done, and how learning actually occurred in his organization. The telling point of this story was that what he saw under both forms of light had virtually no similarity. That is, much of the truly productive activity—the real work and learning—took place in the "white spaces" between the boxes of the organizational chart.

Learning and knowledge transfer also take on a different character within communities of practice. In order to understand this, we must first acknowledge that organizations are fundamentally complex adaptive systems (CAS) (Axelrod and Cohen 1999; Hock 1999; Stacey 2001; Capra 2002; Tuomi 2002; Griffin and Stacey 2005). In order to fully learn something, we must go beyond learning about the subject to become a member of a community where that knowledge lives and is applied in practice. Learning in this way is less about acquiring a certain body of concepts or facts and is more about socialization into a practice community.

Knowledge, too, takes on a different character under this light: It is context-sensitive and dynamic, always changing. It is what Davenport, Prusak and Lesser (Davenport and Prusak 1998; Lesser and Prusak 2004) refer to as "sticky" in that the meaning and relevance of knowledge changes based on the context in which it is used; in short, how it is applied in practice. This is why knowledge management systems that are predicated on storage and retrieval of more or less fixed knowledge assets have proven woefully inadequate in many of today's complex organization environments.

If organizations are fundamentally complex adaptive systems and the knowledge within them is also dynamic and context-sensitive, it follows that our notion of learning and knowledge transfer must also be seen in a new light. We must move from simply learning about something (in a classroom or seminar) to becoming part of the communities where knowledge resides, where it is created, transferred, and applied in practice. We argue that it is in such communities of practice that the most significant forms of learning take place.

Let us return to Rich, our wireless telecommunications manager. What Rich realized, from our work with him, was that while his team members were highly competent, customers were still having a less-than-optimal experience with the service provided, especially during new product and service rollouts. Peculiarly enough, each function within his division appeared to be meeting its targets and metrics. Where the process appeared to be breaking down was not within the functional groups like his, but between the functional areas. In fact, during new product rollouts, members of functional groups that were interdependent on one another for success found themselves embroiled in arguments.

# THE EVOLUTION FROM COP TO ALTS

In order to respond to these challenges, Rich created intentional communities of practice (what we are describing as Action-Learning Teams) to begin working cross-functionally within the "white spaces" to pilot new approaches to working together, solving cross-functional process issues, engaging in intentional knowledge transfer through co-mentoring and cross-training exercises, as well as initiating informal social activities to increase rapport among the functional groups.

An important fact is that many of these activities *had already been occurring in small pockets of Rich's organization based on the initiative of a few members of his team.* What Rich did was recognize, legitimize and provide resources for these activities, thereby increasing their effectiveness and scope. The results were a dramatically reduced deployment cycle for new products and services, fewer errors during deployment, fewer problem ticket escalations from the first-tier support center (due to cross-training and co-mentoring with second-tier support), and dramatically heightened rapport and communication between the functional areas involved.

This story is consistent with scores of other examples from our consulting practice and with significant research conducted on communities of practice within contemporary organizations. Foundations of this research, for example, can be seen in the work of the Xerox Palo Alto Research Center (PARC) headed by Chief Scientist John Seely Brown (Brown and Duguid 2002) and reflected in the work of Etienne Wenger (Wenger 1998; Wenger, McDermott et al. 2002). Recent applications of communities of practice can also be seen in the work of Saint-Onge and Wallace (2003), Verna Allee (1997; 2003) and others (Davenport and Prusak 1998; Lesser, Fontaine et al. 2000; Lesser and Prusak 2004). One consistent principle that stands out from the research is that the more knowledge-intensive and complex the work, the more we rely on informal organizations like communities of practice to be successful.

In order for communities of practice to be successful and fully leveraged to the strategic advantage of the organization, however, they must emerge from obscurity, be given legitimacy and proper resources, and be cultivated as an arm of strategy. They must, in short, evolve into Action-Learning Teams.

# ACTION-LEARNING TEAMS AS AN ARM OF STRATEGY

Action-Learning Teams can be seen as a legitimized and strategically focused form of community of practice; that is, they are recognized for their critical contribution to the organization, provided with necessary resources, focused on strategic-level initiatives, and held accountable for tangible results (LaRue 2005). Like communities of practice, Action-Learning Teams cannot be managed in the traditional sense. They can be cultivated, facilitated, coached, and mentored, but not controlled. As we will see, Action-Learning Teams are also an extremely efficient means of workforce development. Much of the remainder of this book will focus on how to help Action-Learning Teams thrive in your organization, leading to that magical moment where the developmental needs of the worker align with the performance needs of the organization.

# ACTION-LEARNING TEAMS AND THE PRACTICE OF INNOVATION

In their book, *Organizing Genius*, Warren Bennis and Patricia Ward Biederman (1997) provide an insightful analysis of several key innovations produced by teams under extraordinary circumstances. They examined the Manhattan Project, Xerox PARC, Disney, and Lockheed Skunk Works, among others. The teams that were assembled for each of these projects, as well as how they were managed and led, closely resemble how we have characterized Action-Learning Teams.

First, each group was gathered together and guided by a compelling and sometimes awe-inspiring vision, but was left largely to its own devices to determine how to make the vision a reality. Rather than having the task at hand determined for them, these groups had to grapple with just exactly which tasks were necessary to make the vision a reality. While each group was made up of some of the brightest people in their fields, each was engaged in a form of "intellectual boot-strapping," where they were forced to improvise, learn by doing, and create new knowledge and expertise where none had existed before. In short, they had to become Action-Learning Teams.

The level of ambiguity these groups had to deal with on a routine basis would make many of us shudder. They were building bridges into the unknown while walking on them, not knowing exactly where or when they would finally arrive at their elusive destination. Harnessing and guiding the energy of groups like these takes an extraordinary and even sometimes counterintuitive form of leadership. Leaders of Action-Learning Teams must learn to guide—rather than control—the energy of the group to achieve results by tapping into, motivating, and developing the latent talents of knowledge workers. In the next chapter, we will see why learning to organize and lead knowledge workers in this way is quickly becoming the new strategic imperative.

# 7 THE NEW STRATEGIC IMPERATIVE

## SPEED, ADAPTABILITY AND FLEXIBILITY

Under the industrial model of organization, businesses organized themselves along functional lines in order to create long runs of standardized products and services. The role of management under this model was that of grand designer and conductor of the orchestra, and the role of the worker was to follow orders issued by management. The knowledge of the entire end-to-end work process was held strictly in the hands of management.

While this form of organization may have been well-suited for earlier industrial times, today a premium is placed on organizing in a flexible manner that allows firms to create *integrated solutions* for their customers. As competitive pressures intensify and the pace of change quickens, organizations must learn to rapidly respond to market challenges and opportunities in a manner that anticipates the needs and desires of their customers. For these reasons, it is no longer tenable to organize solely along traditional functional lines. Instead, organizations must learn to fluidly collaborate and transfer knowledge across functional boundaries in order to effectively implement desired improvement initiatives.

In addition, businesses increasingly rely on collaboration across multiple organizations, each organization contributing to this process based on its own specialized capability within a complex *value network*. This is the context within which a firm identifies and responds to customers' needs, solves problems, procures input, reacts to competitors, and strives for profit.

# NEW STRATEGIES, NEW STRUCTURES

Action-Learning Teams are groups composed of critical stakeholders in an organization that are tasked with enabling the creation and application of new strategic capabilities and focused on generating a superior end-customer experience. We argue in this chapter that this renewed focus on organizational capabilities that drive integrated customer solutions is quickly becoming the foundation of organizational strategy in the 21$^{st}$ century.

This process is not to be confused with strategic planning, however, as such traditional forms of long-range planning appear ill-suited to today's rapidly changing and competitive marketplace. Rather, we agree with Prahalad and Ramaswamy (2004) that the focus for strategy development today is on building a distinctive set of organizational capabilities that will generate a superior end-customer experience. As Saint-Onge and Wallace (2003) write:

> The model underlying this thinking is that capabilities represent the focal point from which strategies are built. In turn, the organization's performance depends on the quality and reach of its strategies and its ability to provide the necessary individual and organizational capabilities that enable employees to take effective action. (pp. 59-60)

To illustrate how Action-Learning Teams have evolved to this point, we need look no further than the key industries and sectors that have shaped our economy over the past decade or two. We work extensively with organizations in high-tech, wireless voice and data services, pharmaceuticals, biotechnology, aerospace, the Department of Defense, and the like. What these industries and sectors share is an increasing reliance on rapidly evolving network technologies and extremely competitive pressures, both of which drive an ever-increasing pace of change while defying the logic of centralized control. Each of these industries has also shown itself to be increasingly vulnerable to new competitors that seem to arise out of thin air, or from the garage of a tech-savvy entrepreneur.

New government mandates within the Department of Defense are even opening divisions of this historically entrenched bureaucracy to direct competition from private sector organizations. In addition, the new logic of "asymmetric warfare" has created new and formidable challenges to the U.S. Military. See Chapter 11 of this volume and a recent article on the subject (LaRue and Ivany 2004) for more on how the military is responding to these emerging competitive challenges.

Often it is the very structure of these organizations, itself the product of management principles inherited from an earlier era, which inhibits their ability to adapt to change. The key, we believe, lies in the ability of organizations to evolve into much more fluid structures that allow them to adapt more quickly to change, and further, to learn to become change leaders in their industry. Action-Learning Teams represent one such form of fluid, adaptive organization structure that is quickly taking hold in advanced and post-industrial economies where speed, adaptability, and flexibility are becoming the hallmarks of organizational life. We believe that no industry sector will be immune to the pressures we have described here. This is because it takes only one competitor who has learned to organize and apply the collective intelligence of its people to more effectively drive innovation and change. If only one of your competitors learns this process before you do, the very organization you find yourself in today may be gone tomorrow.

In the section that follows, we will tell one such story that emerged in the wireless technology sector. One author of this volume, Kerry Larson, had a front-row seat as a senior executive in a company that helped usher in the wireless revolution. His job, in a nutshell, was to take the ideas of one visionary man, Craig McCaw, and help organize the company in such a way that this vision became a reality, evolving into what is now a nearly ubiquitous facet of modern life.

# ACTION-LEARNING AND THE WIRELESS REVOLUTION

In the early days of McCaw Cellular, this group of young entrepreneurs found itself with an exciting new product, yet were unsure as to how best to market and distribute the new technology. Many felt that cellular telephones would never amount to anything. Investors were suspicious of the profits they were told could be made in the new industry and therefore remained largely on the sidelines. They were unwilling to commit to aggressively funding such a risky and unproven idea largely existing in the vision of one man: Craig McCaw. If the vision became reality, it would have to successfully compete against the established regional telephone companies and also somehow manage its burgeoning debt load.

McCaw Cellular was soon growing rapidly across the country, acquiring properties and spectrum licenses. One of Craig McCaw's favorite sayings was "flexibility is heaven." He despised bureaucracy and realized that creating a company of highly innovative and motivated knowledge workers was the only way to succeed. His strategy was to hire very smart people, share with them the overall goal, and let them figure out the rest. As Kerry Larson, co-author of this book and then senior vice president at McCaw Cellular, recalls:

> We were not sure how best to market this new technology in the various parts of the country and compete with different regional competitors, so we let these smart people figure it out in their part of the country and share with the rest of us what worked and what didn't.

People loved working for McCaw, since they had the freedom to learn and apply their knowledge in the context of real work—in other words; they were engaged in Action-Learning.

As one McCaw veteran recounts, McCaw Cellular had their own version of Action-Learning Teams called "Process Improvement

Teams" or PITs. Despite this unfortunate acronym, these teams had a significant impact on the development of McCaw Cellular. This executive goes on to describe these teams as follows:

> The focus of these teams was usually an area of opportunity (perhaps a process that needed improvement) that had been identified and brought to the attention of the senior management team. Volunteers were solicited to lead and staff the effort with the understanding that the time frame was a bit limited (usually specified but not set in concrete) and that the work would not excuse members from their regular responsibilities. There would not be any additional pay or other compensation. You might think it would have been difficult to find enough volunteers to staff these teams (there were usually two or more teams in existence at any given moment). However, the opposite was true! Employees were quick to volunteer due to the personal satisfaction and notoriety of having been part of a process that improved things in the business.

This philosophy of organization that we have briefly described here helped McCaw become very financially successful, as well as being voted by Washington CEO Magazine as "The Best Company to Work For" three years in a row. McCaw Cellular became the largest independent cellular company in the U.S. before being acquired by AT&T to become AT&T Wireless Services.

Once acquired, the two distinct corporate cultures enjoyed a productive, albeit brief, honeymoon. Soon, however, the more bureaucratic, highly structured, and slow moving culture of AT&T clashed with the flatter, decentralized, and highly entrepreneurial culture of McCaw Cellular. Admittedly, some elements of structure created under the new ownership helped the rapidly growing company streamline and rationalize some of its core processes. For example, under McCaw, the Network Operations Control Centers were regionalized, creating unnecessary redundancies and inconsistent approaches to managing what was becoming a single national wireless network. Under AT&T, these regional control centers were consolidated into one central location, thereby creating a consistent approach while significantly cutting costs.

However, some structural changes imposed by AT&T as well as key leadership changes clearly eroded both the entrepreneurial spirit of McCaw and the company's ability to respond effectively to heightened competition and rapid technological change. AT&T broke the company into traditional functional areas such as Product Development, Marketing, IT, Engineering, and Operations. As new products and services were developed, each functional area was tasked according to its unique functional roles. Each functional area was then subjected to rigorous quality and financial metrics.

At one level, each of these structural and leadership changes made perfect sense. However, at another level of analysis, it quickly became clear that many of these functional areas began to work against one another because each was motivated by different rewards for performance. Product Development and Marketing, for example, were rewarded by a rapid time-to-market, while Engineering and Operations were rewarded according to the quality and performance of the network. In addition, new products and services being rapidly introduced into the network were done so with little regard to their impact on network operations, maintenance, and network bandwidth usage. The result was great fanfare around new product offerings that challenged the network to the extent that the customer experience suffered. At the same time, the explosive growth in popularity of wireless services challenged the company to just be able to keep up with demand for basic services, not to mention new advanced offerings.

The organization under AT&T Wireless became very hierarchical and bureaucratic. Strict protocols of communication and control were introduced. Communication amongst individuals between various ranks in the hierarchy was strictly controlled. All strategic and many operational decisions were made at the top of the organization with little or no input from those who would be affected by the change. Performance Improvement Teams were dismantled. In short, the organization went through a profound cultural change, making the company much more ponderous and unable to quickly respond to the rapid changes occurring in the industry as a whole.

In addition, highly skilled product development teams and engineers at the company began to create scores of new services and gadgetry that, as it turned out, many end users rarely used or even knew existed. On a trip to demonstrate many of these new features and services to the CEO of a major client, one AT&T Wireless vice president remembers the CEO's response: "These features are indeed impressive. Now tell me how they will help me solve the myriad problems I face as I try to manage my global workforce." The VP was rendered nearly speechless. What this customer wanted was not more features and services, but integrated solutions to his problems.

As one executive recounts:

> I think that we ceded our thinking to our vendors in many cases. We were vendor and infrastructure driven, rather than being customer driven. We rolled out new capabilities because we could, not because customers necessarily wanted them or would buy them. I think that this might be an interesting aspect of leadership to explore in terms of managing explosive growth and navigating in times of rapid technological change.

As in many traditional companies, each functional division began to operate as a fiefdom, each fighting for more employees and budget increases. No single consistent knowledge management system was in place to ensure that each functional area was working in concert with all others in furthering company strategy. Instead, a proliferation of various network platforms quickly grew out of control. Ironically, internal measures of efficiency and quality within these functional areas continued largely to meet their targets.

All the while, external industry measures of customer service and satisfaction began to decline. AT&T Wireless launched its "3G" or third generation network by completely overlaying its existing TDMA network in less than two years, which was an astounding accomplishment. However, the full deployment of the next-generation, high-speed voice and data services, that would have kept the company technologically competitive, was inconsistent in various regions across the country, and the entire process began to slow.

Despite the most successful IPO in history when AT&T Wireless finally broke off from AT&T in 2001, the company was soon in decline, with a culture much more similar to the parent AT&T than that of its roots of McCaw. The rest, as they say, is history. As we write this, AT&T Wireless is now under new ownership by its former rival, Cingular Wireless.

Certainly, the decline of AT&T Wireless occurred at a time when there was an overall shift in the economy away from the technology sector in general and wireless in particular. However, we would argue that, as the wireless industry began to reach maturity, *all firms* in the sector predictably faced shrinking margins and intensified competition, leaving those companies with superior organizational capabilities better positioned to emerge as leaders during industry consolidation.

# IMPLICATIONS FOR THE ROAD AHEAD

As we can begin to see from the story above, in order for employees to take effective action, they must clearly understand their role within the context of the strategic direction of the organization and the various functions charged with implementing this strategy. Once the strategic direction and their role within it is clear, the focus of the Action-Learning Team must shift to identifying critical process gaps and behavioral barriers that stand between where we are and where we intend to be as an organization. We must further understand that, more often than not, the most critical behavior and process gaps exist between rather than within functional areas of the organization, and thus any attempts to close these gaps must address the critical issue of cross-functional communication and alignment.

Once these gaps are identified, they must be prioritized and focus placed on creating the capabilities necessary to close the gaps and accomplish the strategy. We propose that one of the most efficient ways of closing these gaps is through the formation of Action-Learning Teams that are explicitly charged with developing the capabilities we have identified, and launching initiatives that directly support this strategy. As we have seen in the above example, these teams must also be sanctioned at a level in the organization commensurate with the task they are asked to perform, i.e., they must be given authority to take action.

## STRUCTURES THAT MIRROR THE COMPLEXITY OF THEIR ENVIRONMENT

We can also see from the example above that, to achieve dominance within a sector such as wireless technology where rapid change and competition are the order of the day, internal organizational structure must mirror the complexities of their external environment. Known as "requisite variety," this principle simply states that an organism's capacity to adapt to a changing fitness landscape depends on the ability of its internal structures to keep pace with the complexity of its environment. For our purposes, this means that any organization, which is in the end a complex adaptive system, must evolve and sustain internal structures that are inherently adaptive and flexible.

Arguably, some additional structure imposed by AT&T was necessary to allow McCaw Cellular to reduce internal redundancies and inefficiencies and to create alignment among its various regional divisions. However, these additional structures along with a top down leadership hierarchy proved to be too burdensome and did not allow the new firm to quickly respond to the competitive pressures and technological change in the market environment.

In the chapter that follows, we will take you on a journey into the rise of the knowledge worker and the profound implications this new breed of worker has for organizational leadership and change.

# 8 LEADING EFFECTIVE ACTION-LEARNING TEAMS

In this chapter, we will explore the profound shift in leadership and organizational culture emerging largely as a result of new technologies that defy the logic of centralized control. We will demonstrate how this shift is having a profound impact on nearly every aspect of our culture and society, not least of which are modern organizations.

## LEADING FROM A DIFFERENT PLACE

We argue that the fusion of information and communication technologies has set in motion a world that defies the logic of centralized control. While the politics of our nation states learned this lesson all too well, perhaps best exemplified by the disintegration of the Soviet Union and the fall of the Berlin Wall, modern organizations have been a bit slower in their transition away from command and control systems of governance.

While we must arguably maintain certain positions in organizations where accountability for achieving results ultimately resides, the means by which we achieve these results must surely evolve in order to more fully utilize the intelligence that exists at all levels of the organization. Leaders who understand this necessity must begin to move away from the need to control and provide detailed road maps for their organizations toward creating the optimal context for this new form of "distributed intelligence" to evolve (see Chapter 11). They must learn to move away from strategic planning toward developing the ability to clearly communicate their "strategic intent," or the direction the organization is to move. As Pascale, Millemann, and Gioja (1997) write:

> Leading from a different place also entails a transformation in the operating state of leaders themselves. They become a microcosm of the shift in vital signs that they want to see in their organizations. From resigning themselves to the limits of their power to make things happen (and to the implausibility of expecting middle managers to help), they move toward the possibility of genuinely distributed intelligence; from taking on an identity as the person in charge, they become clearinghouses for the different ways an enrolled organization handles its responsibilities; from avoiding straight talk, they develop an ability to handle and even encourage constructive conflict; from assuming that they must provide a detailed road map for the journey, they begin to accept learning as a form of inquiry in action. (p. 135)

# ORGANIZATIONAL STRUCTURE, CULTURE, AND LEADERSHIP

So just what organizational culture and structure must leaders create in order to best promote distributed intelligence and Action-Learning? While many organizations are of necessity beginning to move in this direction, we would like to offer a slightly radical yet extremely successful example of a form of organizational structure and leadership that has led to a genuine form of distributed intelligence.

No single organization has captured our imagination in this regard quite like VISA. It handles a volume of $1.25 trillion and has grown 20-50 percent compounded annually for the past 30 years. Its products have successfully transcended national, cultural, and religious boundaries to become a truly global currency. Yet its organizational structure and system of governance has remained largely a mystery. Even when one looks under the hood, the concepts are highly counterintuitive in light of modern business practices, yet in many respects they could not be simpler or closer to the organization of nature itself. According to VISA founder Dee Hock (1999), the lessons to be learned here are profound— and critical to the survival of all modern enterprise.

Hock, an unemployed banker at the time, wandered the forests of the Pacific Northwest reflecting on the implications of the emerging science of "Complexity" for the structure and leadership of modern business. Influenced by the work of the Santa Fe Institute, the concept that emerged for him he would later call the "chaordic organization," meaning an intelligent nexus of chaos and order. Hock believes, with some significant justification, that modern organizations must shed their Industrial Age thinking to incorporate chaordic principles or risk going the way of the dinosaur. He writes (1999):

> Today, before any audience in the world, I can hold a VISA card overhead and ask, "How many of you recognize this?" Every hand in the room will go up. When I ask, "How many of you can tell me who owns it, where it's headquartered, how it operates, or where to buy shares?" a dead silence comes over the room. The audience realizes something extraordinary has occurred, and they haven't a clue how it happened. Nor, in my judgment, should they: The results of the best organizations are apparent, but the structure, leadership, and process are transparent....(pp. 189-191)

Today, twenty-nine years later, its products are created by 22,000 owner-member financial institutions and accepted at 15 million merchant locations in more than 200 countries and territories. Three-quarters of a billion people use VISA products to make 14 billion transactions producing annual volume of $1.25 trillion – the single largest block of consumer purchasing power in the global economy. VISA has grown a minimum of 20 percent and as much as 50 percent compounded annually for three decades, through the best and the worst of times, with no end in sight.

The entirety, like millions of other chaordic organizations, including those we call body, brain, forest, ocean, and biosphere, was largely self-regulating....Today, those systems clear more electronic financial transactions in a week than the U.S. Federal Reserve system does in a year....

Time and time again, they demonstrated a simple truth we have somehow lost sight of in our mechanistic, Industrial Age, command-and-control organizations: The truth is that, given the right chaordic circumstances, from no more than dreams, determination, and the liberty to try, quite ordinary people consistently do extraordinary things.

# CHARACTERISTICS OF AN ACTION-LEARNING TEAM LEADER

So what lessons about leadership can we learn from VISA and from other examples outlined in this book? The characteristics of an ALT leader are a combination of business resolve and the ability to effectively facilitate a team to achieve positive results. Depending on the culture of the organization, an Action-Learning Team leader may also need to have formal position power in order to have access and influence on the rest of the organization. The most critical characteristics of an Action-Learning Team leader are as follows:

- Builds on the Wisdom and Insight of the Team
- Models the Change They Seek in the Organization
- High Level of Trust and Respect By and For the Team
- Leverages Ambiguity to Drive Innovation
- Focuses Group through Clarity of Intent

- Adapts Leadership Style to the Situation
- Exercises *Soft-Focus* and Pattern Recognition
- Promotes Culture of Freedom and Accountability

# BUILDS ON THE WISDOM AND INSIGHT OF THE TEAM

In the beginning stages of forming an Action-Learning Team, especially in the phase we call "Inquiry," the leader should be questioning, probing, summarizing, and establishing norms of behavior. The leader must create a space for the team to reflect and assess the situation and the appropriateness of various solutions, and not to become wedded to a particular course of action too early. Later, the leader needs to bring together the thoughts, ideas, and learning of the team to a point of action, while continually encouraging the team to test and refine the chosen course of action based on its ability to achieve desired results.

# MODELS THE CHANGE THEY SEEK IN THE ORGANIZATION

The leader of an Action-Learning Team must create a microcosm of the change they seek in the organization by modeling the behavior and mind-set they desire. Jim Collins' (2001) description of the characteristics of a Level 5 leader in his book *Good to Great: Why some companies make the leap – and others don't* closely parallels that of an ALT leader: We believe that the more the leader models these behaviors, the greater the chance that the Action-Learning Team will develop these same characteristics. We have summarized Collins' characteristics of Level 5 leaders as follows:

**Humility** – Acts with quiet, calm determination. Relies on inspired standards, not charisma to motivate.
**Professional Will** – Is a catalyst for superb results.
**Modesty** – Is modest and doesn't seek public adulation. Not boastful.
**Resolve** – Demonstrates unwavering resolve. Does whatever it takes to produce long-term results.
**Determination** – Sets the standard in getting quality results. Settles for nothing less.

Collins suggests that Level 5 leaders already exist in most organizations. He suggests looking for situations where extraordinary results exist, yet no individual steps forth to claim the credit. Level 5 leaders practice self-reflection, have had significant life experience, and normally have had the benefit of working under a great boss or mentor. They also tend to be developed from within organizations rather than being brought in from the outside.

We believe that Action-Learning Teams, if led wisely by leaders who model these behaviors, can be an excellent incubator for Level 5 leaders.

# HIGH LEVEL OF TRUST AND RESPECT BY AND FOR THE TEAM

High levels of trust and mutual respect are hallmarks of Action-Learning Teams. If team members fear reprisal, they will not share their insights, thoughts, or criticisms freely, and the team will not achieve the results they desire.

In general, criticism should be framed in terms of specific, observable behaviors or actions, and not directed at individuals personally. In other words, criticize behaviors and not people. In addition, criticism should be reinforced with specific suggestions for future improvement. Marshall Goldsmith (Goldsmith 2003; Goldsmith, Morgan et al. 2004) refers to this as offering "feed-forward" rather than "feedback." This keeps the group centered on constructive suggestions rather than allowing these conversations to degrade the climate of the group.

# LEVERAGES AMBIGUITY TO DRIVE INNOVATION

Often, our natural response to ambiguity is to eliminate it as soon as possible. But ambiguity can be a powerful force for innovation if we learn to tolerate and even embrace it. As Pascale et al. write, "Leaders must place themselves squarely in the zone of discomfort and learn to tolerate ambiguity" (p. 135). With ambiguity comes potential, possibility, and options for action. Once we decide on a course of action, we eliminate ambiguity, as well as many of our options. Leaders of Action-Learning Teams must model the ability to tolerate ambiguity in the early stages of a project or initiative, and not allow the group to come to premature closure on a course of action. Once a course of action is determined, leaders must not allow the group to become too wedded to their scripts, and to exploit hidden opportunities that inevitably emerge.

# FOCUSES GROUP THROUGH CLARITY OF INTENT

As we can see in this and the contribution by Robert Ivany (see Chapter 11), commanders have learned to issue clear and concise statements of intent (or purpose) that give maximum freedom of action to subordinates in terms of how to accomplish their mission. This is similar to a principle outlined by Gareth Morgan (1997) mentioned earlier as the principle of "minimum critical specifications" where we "...define no more than is absolutely necessary" to launch a given initiative or activity (p. 103). Morgan goes on:

> They have to avoid the role of "grand designer" in favor of one that focuses on facilitation, orchestration, and boundary management, creating "enabling conditions" that allow a system to find its own form. The challenge is to help operating units, whether they be spin-off businesses, work teams, research groups, or individuals, find and operate within a sphere of "bounded" or "responsible autonomy." The challenge is to avoid the anarchy and the completely free flow that arises when there are no parameters or guidelines, on the one hand, and over-centralization, on the other. (p. 114)

As Robert Ivany writes, in Chapter 11 of this volume, we are all increasingly living in a volatile, uncertain, complex, and ambiguous (or VUCA) world. It is up to the leader to model not only how to cope with this new environment, but to leverage the opportunities that come with this new world to our advantage.

# ADAPTS LEADERSHIP STYLE TO THE SITUATION

Known as "situational leadership," a term coined by Paul Hersey (1985), this principle simply states that there should be no prescription without diagnosis. While this may seem obvious, how often have we been susceptible to the management trend of the month where we are persuaded to believe that the author has discovered the one right way to manage? How often have consultants come into your office with a solution in search of a problem? It is as if these people do not actually "see" you or your situation in all its subtleties, they do not "hear" your explanations or concerns, but instead they see you and your situation through the lens of their preconceived methodologies, tools, techniques, and, of course, sales quotas.  They have a proverbial hammer in their hand and everything looks like a nail.

Situational leadership helps us recognize that every situation is unique, requiring us to become aware of our own biases, preconceptions, and prejudices as we encounter each new circumstance.  As leaders, we need to remain flexible, recognize and exploit unforeseen opportunities as they arise, and adapt our leadership style accordingly.  Obviously, if the ship is sinking, we are not going to call a committee meeting.  In a crisis, subordinates must simply follow orders without hesitation.  In the absence of an acute crisis, however, leaders must have an expanded repertoire of approaches and methods at their disposal designed to draw out the wisdom and insights of their team.

# EXERCISES SOFT-FOCUS AND PATTERN RECOGNITION

Regardless of our position in our organization, we must all learn to see our actions within their broader context.  As Robert Ivany, former President of the U.S. Army War College puts it, "tactical decisions have strategic consequences" (LaRue and Ivany 2004).  Unless we recognize how our actions relate to the broader whole, whether this is the vision of the organization or our vision for our own lives, we run the risk of making short-term tactical decisions that run counter to our long-term values and goals.

As the pace of change quickens and the world grows in complexity, we are faced with an ever-expanding array of potential choices, and the law of unforeseen consequences tells us these choices will in turn impact a greater number of those around us in ways we cannot predict in advance. All the while, we are expected to demonstrate decisiveness in the face of this increasing uncertainty and ambiguity.  But uncertainty and ambiguity breed anxiety, and anxiety too often compels us to be reactive, putting out fires and treating symptoms rather than finding high leverage points that can create lasting change. Under these circumstances, action is too often valued over thoughtful reflection. Soft-focus can help us locate hidden patterns in the barrage of events we face on a daily basis in order to gain maximum leverage from our choices.

The term *Soft-Focus* comes from Linda Shaffer-Vanaria, a former Navy squadron commander and test pilot turned executive coach. Linda realizes more than most that fixating on details can get you killed in a heartbeat. "If you become hard-focused on one thing," she writes, "other things can run away from you. The fighter pilot must remain aware of their environment in its totality at all times. There is a constant barrage of information that must remain within your scan—pilot jargon for keeping a strategically timed eye on everything important. The scope of required awareness includes threat and surroundings, the readings of our instrument panel, the overall "feel" of our aircraft, how the mission as a whole is progressing, how others in our formation are doing, as well as our own capacity as a pilot to perform. We must connect all of these dots and hold the big picture in focus in "real time". The best pilots understand this intuitively." (LaRue 2005, p. 7)

Why the pilot experiences are so meaningful is that they speak to environments with high degrees of complexity and rapid rates of change. Our businesses and lives are all growing more complex as time goes on. They may not be as dramatic as that of the fighter pilot but the principals of soft focus are the same.

Soft-focus is a discipline that helps our decisions to be informed by the "view from the canopy," helping to ensure that today's choices take us where we want to be tomorrow. Soft-Focus is a form of "reflection-in-action" that allows us to leverage ambiguity to drive innovation. Soft-Focus helps us to recognize patterns in events and determine where to put our organizational "crowbar" in order to achieve maximum leverage for our effort. Soft-Focus teaches us not to become too wedded to our favorite scripts, or to allow our goals or current vision to become blinders that prevent us from identifying unforeseen opportunities and fresh alternatives for action that may not be immediately evident.

# PROMOTES CULTURE OF FREEDOM AND ACCOUNTABILITY

As is often said of democracy: with freedom comes responsibility. As leaders, our main responsibility is to define where we are going and what needs to be done, leaving maximum freedom and flexibility to our subordinates as to how to accomplish our intent. Nonetheless, with freedom comes accountability for achieving intended outcomes in the most efficient manner possible. This means that it is incumbent upon subordinates to clarify, when necessary, the intent of the leader, the boundaries within which they must act, and how their actions fit into the larger whole of the organization.

As we will see in the next chapter, complexity and rapid change have given rise to the knowledge worker, a unique breed of worker that must be managed like a volunteer in order to fully leverage their talents and abilities. No one is quite certain what will arise as a result of organizations that are structured and led in such a way that they draw out and fully utilize the competencies of knowledge workers. One thing is certain, however: While we can command compliance, commitment is voluntary.

# 9 ACTION-LEARNING TEAMS AND KNOWLEDGE WORKER DEVELOPMENT

## THE RISE OF THE KNOWLEDGE WORKER

Peter Drucker (1999; 2002), who is credited with coining the term "knowledge worker," draws a stark contrast between industrial and knowledge work. In the industrial model of production, particularly under the influence of Frederick Winslow Taylor (1856-1915), workers were programmed by their task in isolated, repetitive, and highly routine jobs. In many respects, the role of humans in early industrial production foreshadowed that of robotics in later industrial times. Workers were never asked the question, "What is your task?" Instead, the task was determined for them by management, and the only question was, "How can the task best be performed?" Thus, the problem of how to make industrial workers more productive was framed in terms of capital investment in plant and equipment, and in simplifying the work process to make workers more interchangeable and replaceable.

Lest you think that Taylor and the method of scientific management he created should be relegated to the historical pages of an era gone by, we should consider Drucker's (1999) words:

> "Scientific Management" (and its successor, "Industrial Engineering") is the one American philosophy that has swept the world—more so even than the Constitution and the Federalist Papers. In the last century there has been only one worldwide philosophy that could compete with

Taylor's: Marxism. And in the end, Taylor has triumphed over Marx. (p. 139)

In addition, the concept of industrial workers collaborating was often construed as conspiring against management and was routinely discouraged on the shop floor. Knowledge of the entire end-to-end production process resided with management, and the role of management was predicated on maintaining their hold on this knowledge (see, for example, the classic study by Zuboff 1988). However, this state of affairs was about to change in ways that we are just now beginning to come to terms with in advanced capitalist economies such as the United States.

As the pace of technological change quickened, and especially with the burgeoning of information and communication technologies that defied the logic of centralized control, the once-routine tasks of the industrial worker began to transform.

First, the internal logic of capitalism and global trade meant that any job that could be eliminated through automation or shipped overseas to lower-wage countries soon met its fate. Likening capitalism to blood pressure, capital tends to flow to where the pressure is lowest in terms of labor, environmental, and other regulatory and social costs. Second, the jobs that remained became more highly specialized, requiring more formal education and sophisticated training.

Today, one of the defining characteristics of a knowledge worker is that they know far more about their job than their manager. In addition, knowledge workers are not programmed by specified tasks. Instead, we must often ask the question of knowledge workers: "What is your task? What should it be? What should you be expected to contribute?" and, "What hampers you in doing your task and should be eliminated?" (Drucker 1999, p. 138)

Third, knowledge workers at the very least have a symbiotic relationship with their employer: The employer often needs the knowledge worker as much as the knowledge worker needs the employer. Today, knowledge workers possess the highly portable skills and collaborative learning networks that transcend organizational boundaries. This state of affairs is unprecedented in history. The power and authority of the capitalist in earlier times was predicated on the ownership of capital and control of the means of production. Today, knowledge workers increasingly own both. In terms of capital, knowledge workers increasingly control the largest single block of funds traded on Wall Street in the form of pension and mutual funds. In terms of the means of production, knowledge workers own the most valuable real estate in an organization—the space between their ears. It is therefore up to employers to create environments that attract and continuously develop the best knowledge workers.

# DEVELOPING KNOWLEDGE WORKERS

Robert Kegan (Kegan 1994; Kegan and Lahey 2001) compared contemporary work to family systems literature, which led him to the insight that traditional organizations have perpetuated a rather unfortunate state of affairs where managers behave as unwitting parents and employees as adolescents who never grow up to become accountable, responsible adults.

While this state of affairs may have served us well in earlier industrial times, when a premium was placed on unquestioning obedience and routine tasks, the opposite is true today. As the title of his book suggests, we are *In Over Our Heads*. Our average developmental level today lagging far behind what is required of us to be successful – both as individuals and organizations. Kegan summed up the traits of an effective worker today as "acting like an owner" rather than as an entitled, dependent employee. We can see these traits in more detail in the table that follows.

*Table 2: The New Mental Demands of Modern Work. Adapted from Kegan (1994, p. 302)*

| TODAY'S DEMANDS | YESTERDAY'S DEMANDS |
|---|---|
| Be the inventor or owner of our work; distinguish our work from our job | See work as owned and created by the employer |
| Be self-initiating, self-correcting, and self-evaluating | Be dependent on others to frame the problems, initiate adjustments, and determine whether things are going acceptably well |
| Be guided by our own visions at work | Be without a vision or be captive of the authority's agenda |
| Take responsibility for what happens to us at work externally and internally | See our present internal circumstances and future external possibilities as caused by someone else |
| Be accomplished masters of our particular jobs or careers | Have an apprenticing or imitating relationship to what we do |
| Conceive of the organization from the "outside in," as a whole; see our relation to the whole; see the relation of the parts to the whole | See the rest of the organization and its parts only from the perspective of our own part from the "inside out" |

Action-Learning Teams are an effective means of creating the owner's mentality by combining a culture of empowerment with an enhanced capability to design and implement change. Managers who have a tendency toward control are taught to become effective facilitators, mentors and coaches, while employees with a tendency toward passivity are taught to become involved partners and co-creators in the change process. Both managers and workers must learn to see themselves less in terms of their particular functional roles and more as members of the whole, each with an integral role to play in the design and implementation of change.

# WHY TRAINING IS NOT ENOUGH

Much is said today about empowerment and being self-directed. However, as we will see, the hidden demands of self-direction imply the ability to remove oneself from the immediate demands of one's functional role to view one's activities in relation to the larger organizational context. It appears, however, that viewing oneself within the context of the larger systemic environment is only the first step.

That is, as we will see in Chapter 11, it is not enough for soldiers preparing for battle to comprehend the strategy as formulated by their superiors, regardless of how comprehensive their initial understanding may be. It is the element of surprise, the craftiness and unpredictability of their opponents, which demands of them the ability to improvise, to make sense of the data of the battlefield as it emerges, and to quickly formulate new action strategies based on this new understanding.

The sheer speed at which this improvised reformulation must take place, the volume of data, the innumerable shifting variables of battle, and the unpredictability of their opponents make the routing of such decisions through central command an untenable option. As we have argued, the competitive marketplace that serves as the economic battlefield for today's worker differs from this scenario only in degree. Decisions and strategies reserved for the managerial and professional ranks are moving to the periphery of the organization, as is the need for critical, often improvisational judgment and thinking. The ability to theorize, to rapidly construct working hypotheses based on relationships among rapidly changing data, which themselves must be selectively drawn from a myriad of sources, is now becoming the foundational competency of knowledge work.

In sum, it is no longer sufficient to understand any particular system for "sense-making," but it is increasingly necessary to develop the ability to construct such systems as shifting circumstances warrant. This capability lies at the heart of Action-Learning.

Further, we now know that due to unprecedented levels of specialization, much of knowledge work must of necessity occur in groups and in teams. This is because complex tasks require the concerted, coordinated effort of multiple specialists. We believe, therefore, that Action-Learning Teams hold the greatest promise for the development of knowledge work competencies. We wrote this book in order to help leaders and knowledge workers alike learn to better understand the dynamics of these teams and how best to cultivate them to the advantage of both knowledge workers and the organization as a whole.

# KNOWLEDGE, BASIC ASSUMPTIONS, AND AWARENESS

We can now begin to see that what we understand by the term "knowledge" in relation to today's work environment is far from a state of fixed propositions and structures that hold true irrespective of circumstance. To internalize and act according to such structures is likened to what Kegan termed the "third order of consciousness." That is, people who operate at this level of awareness tend not to question the assumptions that underlie their thinking.

Kegan argues that most models of learning either view worker deficits in terms of a dependency which must be excised, or an information deficit conceived in terms of a lack of skills or knowledge which must be imparted to the worker (1994, p. 163). However, a perceived overdependence on authority figures or gaps in skill or knowledge may, in Kegan's view, be symptomatic of a structure of consciousness ill-equipped to cope with the demands of the contemporary workplace. This structure, which he termed the "third order of consciousness," was characterized by the apprehension of a system of thought from within that system. In other words, those who operate at the third order tend not to be aware of the presuppositions and assumptions that underlie their thinking.

A person could conceivably be a Nobel Laureate in their chosen field and continue to operate at the third order of consciousness. As Peter Drucker (1999) points out, basic assumptions create the unconscious boundaries within which thinking takes place:

> BASIC ASSUMPTIONS ABOUT REALITY are the PARADIGMS of a social science, such as management. They are usually held subconsciously by the scholars, the writers, the teachers, the practitioners in the field. Yet those assumptions largely determine what the discipline— scholars, writers, teachers, practitioners—assumes to be REALITY. (p. 3)

The discipline of innovation—and we do argue in this book that it is a discipline that can be cultivated—requires that individuals and groups routinely question the assumptions that limit their thinking. We must move from what Kegan and Lahey (2001) refer to as "assumptions that hold us" to "assumptions we hold." That is, we must become aware of and test the validity of our assumptions in order to expand the boundaries of what we think is possible.

The late physicist David Bohm (Bohm 1994; Bohm and Nichol 1996) thought that the discipline of uncovering and systematically questioning one's basic assumptions was so critical to the survival and development of humankind that he devoted the later years of his life to this effort. Following the development of the atom bomb, he realized that humans were capable of wielding their technological sword for both malevolent and benevolent purposes, based largely on intentions of which they were only partially aware. These unconscious intentions often became hidden within the fabric of culture, creating a system of thought (and subsequent action) that lay just below the threshold of awareness. He believed that, as humans learned to awaken from the unconscious hold of these assumptions, they could learn to expand the realm of the possible while living their lives with greater clarity and conscious intent.

In this sense, learning is less about imparting a certain content of knowledge and is more about uncovering and testing the limits of the assumptions that define our knowledge. Should such enduring structures of knowledge exist, we would have found ourselves in the rather enviable position of simply imparting such stable structures through the process of basic education or training. Instead, workers today are being called to routinely uncover and question their own assumptions about the relevance of the task at hand as well as how best to perform that task within the context of the strategic intent of the organization.

To illustrate how important it is for knowledge workers to understand the strategic context within which their work takes place, consider the comments of the physicist Richard Feynman as recounted by Warren Bennis and Patricia Ward Biederman (1997, p. 205) from their research on the Manhattan Project. Feynman recounts the following critical turning point in the Manhattan Project as follows:

> The army had recruited talented engineers and others from all over the United States for special duty on the project. They were assigned to work on the primitive computers of the period, doing energy calculations and other tedious jobs. But the army, obsessed with security, refused to tell them anything specific about the project. They didn't know that they were building a weapon that could end the war or

even what their calculations meant. They were simply expected to do the work, which they did—slowly and not very well.

Feynman, who supervised the technicians, prevailed on his superiors to tell the recruits what they were doing and why. Permission was granted to lift the veil of secrecy, and Oppenheimer gave them a special lecture on the nature of the project and their own contribution. "Complete transformation," Feynman recalled that they began to invent ways of doing it better. They improved the scheme. They worked at night. They didn't need supervising in the night; they didn't need anything. They understood everything; they invented several of the programs that we used.

Ever the scientist, Feynman calculated that the work was done "nearly ten times as fast" after it had meaning.

# THE CORE ATTRIBUTES OF KNOWLEDGE WORK

Developing the owners' mentality, understanding the strategic context of our work, learning to question our basic assumptions, learning to define the appropriateness of a given task as well as how best to perform our work, learning to improvise, reflect, tap into and enhance the collective wisdom of our colleagues—these are the basic attributes of knowledge work. These capabilities, taken as a whole and applied in practice within the context of collaborative work, describe in essence the role of Action-Learning Teams in organizations. In other words, Action-Learning Teams are groups composed of knowledge workers who share a common purpose in the development of themselves, their team, and their organization through the application of knowledge.

As we have argued, traditional forms of training and education are simply incapable of developing these competencies. In the section that follows, we will look in depth at a real-life example of how organizations are being forced to abandon well-worn paths of worker development in favor of more novel approaches, while increasing individual accountability for learning and dismantling the traditional barriers that stand in the way of innovation and change.

# FROM TRAINING TO LEARNING IN ACTION

Jenny, an internal organizational consultant for a multinational corporation with a well-established corporate university system, expressed her company's frustration with their more traditional approach to training and how it fostered dependent forms of behavior. Although their corporate university was lauded in the business press for its best practices and was well-suited to deliver training aimed at very narrow problems or skill gaps, it was not nearly dynamic enough to remain current with systemic or strategic issues which varied according to the needs of different sectors in her company.

More importantly, however, such tactical learning did not address dependent forms of behavior that tended to undermine the workers' accountability for their own learning and development process.

The initiative, spearheaded by the company's CEO, was based on six basic questions asked of employees at all levels of the organization (LaRue 1999, p. 109):

- Do you have a substantive, meaningful job?
- Do you have the knowledge and skills you need to be successful?

- Has training been identified and made available to you?
- Do you have a career plan?
- Do you get feedback on a regular basis?
- Is your workplace bias-free?

Jenny (LaRue 1999) summarized the key elements of the initiative as follows:

> Basically, it's a performance process that's driven by the employee. The manager's role is to create an environment that supports the employee's success and create an environment of mentoring and coaching. The employees set their own goals based on the strategic plans for the organization, so that they link their goals to those plans. "What do I have to do to help my organization be successful?" They identify work partners that are affected by the work they do, who can give them feedback. They identify behaviors that are critical to helping them achieve their goals. Then they meet on a quarterly basis with a manager to talk about their results, how they've demonstrated the behaviors and how those behaviors have helped them achieve their goals. They get feedback from their work partners on a quarterly basis. (p. 111)

Although the initiative was designed to empower employees in determining skill and development gaps while defining custom solutions to these gaps through a mentoring relationship with supervisors, the initiative as it was originally conceived failed completely. According to Jenny, there were two major reasons for this failure. First:

> Managers thought it was a very threatening thing, because if people answered 'no' to any of those questions, they saw it as something that someone could come back and beat them up with. So they encouraged employees, to the point of intimidation, to answer all questions 'yes.'

She elaborated further:

> When we first rolled this out, I had senior-level executives tell me in training sessions, "I don't know how to talk to my people this way! I tell my people what to do, but I don't ask them what they need!" They had no training. They didn't understand the whole concept of two-way, level playing field dialogue.

The second reason was that there is often a payoff to dependent behavior in organizations that, in Jenny's words (LaRue 1999), took the following form:

> I think we have a lot of employees who don't want that control over their own destiny, because they really like being able to say, "Well, they did it to me." They're not going to want to take control of their own destiny, as it were, within the work environment either. There's going to be some resistance on both sides of it. (p. 112)

There are several key points we would like to emphasize about this initiative that are central to the present work. First, in order to be successful, this initiative needed to address what we, borrowing from Kegan, have referred to as the "hidden curriculum" of self-direction:

1. Workers are increasingly being called upon to make decisions and formulate actions based on a systemic understanding of their work context.
2. The institutional barriers to this form of work and learning must be identified and dismantled if workers are to be successful in this new role.

On the first point, consider again a key element of this strategy: "The employees set their own goals based on the strategic plans for the organization, so that they linked their goals to those plans." The very ability of workers to accomplish the objectives set forth in this initiative was therefore predicated on a systemic understanding of the organization and its strategy. To accomplish this, Jenny (LaRue 1999) had this to say about the development of the competencies of self-directed learning:

> One of the things that I have done with our training organization within the sector is to partner with them on some projects, particularly around self-directed learning. We have taken them to the top for a more strategic thinking level and got them to look at the overall corporate objective and how they, as trained professionals, can impact those strategic objectives through their self-directed learning programs. So, it's not necessarily about what they do, but about how they do it and how they approach their work. (p. 113)

Rather than viewing workers as passive individuals suffering from a deficit of knowledge or skill to be alleviated by the educator or trainer, the approach outlined by this individual demonstrates how the learner and their relationship to knowledge must both undergo transformation. Robert Kegan (1994) framed the problem in a very similar manner:

> An informational stance leaves the form as it is and focuses on changing what people know; it is essentially a training model for personal change. I would contrast this with a transformational stance, which places the form itself at risk for change and focuses on changes in how people know…While training increases the fund of knowledge, education leads us out of or liberates us from one construction or organization of mind in favor of a larger one. (pp. 163-164)

# LESSONS LEARNED FROM THE CORPORATE UNIVERSITY

We can see from the story above that it is not enough to create a self-directed learning environment, even one with access to a fully-funded corporate university system. What we believe is missing from this equation is that we must first uncover and test the relevance of our assumptions about learning and knowledge transfer in light of the complexities of the modern workplace. We must overcome pervasive attitudes of dependency and parochialism in order for workers to appropriately direct their own learning within a broader understanding of the work context. Additionally, while self-directed learning is a powerful concept, the approach taken by this organization (like too many others we encounter) failed to leverage the power of informal *communities of practice* and what we call *Action-Learning Teams*.

Finally, we must also identify and remove long-standing cultural barriers to learning and self-direction: namely the threat these pose to traditional management and authority structures. Traditional managers—and our workplaces are still full of them—are simply uncomfortable with the notion of workers questioning "how things are done around here" (LaRue 1999, p. 164).

In the chapter that follows, we will take you on a journey into the foundations of Action-Learning in order to help you see just why this evolving discipline is so crucial to the development of a truly learning organization.

# 10 THE ACTION CONTEXT AS LEARNING ENVIRONMENT

A highly unfortunate consequence of the Industrial Era that continues to cloud our perception of the present reality is the distinction between theoretical and practical knowledge. While this distinction may have served society adequately in a de-skilled Taylorist workplace, this carefully guarded, even hallowed distinction has become dangerously sanctimonious in the age of the knowledge worker (LaRue 1999; LaRue 2002; LaRue and Sobol 2002).

## THE ROLE OF CONTEXT IN LEARNING

While the term "vocational" has been used to describe workers in the industrial era, we are finding that the term "professional" most closely characterizes the knowledge worker of the present. What the two terms hold in common, however, is the central role of the context in their learning process. The former Soviet psychologist Lev Vygotsky (1986) developed an elegant social-psychological theory of activity predicated largely on the interaction of humans with their psychosocial surround. Vygotsky's theory offered an action-oriented alternative to the dominant theory of the time spearheaded in the west by Jean Piaget (1977), which followed a more linear and deterministic stage approach to development. Piaget's framework left little room for the role of activity and context in the developmental process.

For thinkers like Gregory Bateson (1979), on the other hand, context is the crucial and indispensable element for the development of all life forms at all levels in both biological and social terms:

> Without context, words and actions have no meaning at all. This is true not only of human communication in words, but also of all communication whatsoever, of all mental process, of all mind, including that which tells the sea anemone how to grow and the amoeba what he should do next. (p. 15)

In terms of Western educational practice, the central role of context in the learning process has its roots perhaps most notably in the writings of John Dewey. As Dewey explained (1916, Chapter 23), one's "calling" is the primary vehicle through which one's experience is apprehended and meaningful context is created:

> A calling is...of necessity an organizing principle for information and ideas; for knowledge and intellectual growth. It provides an axis which runs through an immense diversity of detail; it causes different experiences, facts, items of information to fall into order with one another. The lawyer, the physician, the laboratory investigator in some branch of chemistry, the parent, the citizen interested in his own locality, has a constant working stimulus to note and relate whatever has to do with his concern. He unconsciously, from the motivation of his occupation, reaches out for all relevant information, and holds to it. The vocation acts as both magnet to attract and as glue to hold.

Dewey's philosophy, known as instrumentalism, holds that knowledge is a function of inquiry. "Truth" therefore is an instrument for solving problems, and hence changes as problems and situations change. According to this view, truth, being devoid of any transcendent quality, cannot be fully discerned in the absence of experience. Pure thought or reason is incomplete of itself, and is completed only through experience which informs it, confirming or denying its validity. As Dewey said (1916, Chapter 11), "An ounce of experience is better than a ton of theory simply because it is only in experience that any theory has vital and verifiable significance."

For Dewey, the segmenting of education into two distinct components of theory and practice carries far-reaching implications. The consequences of this dichotomy are only magnified due to the increased cognitive demands of today's workplace which assume a firm foundation of experience and actual practice (Dewey, 1916, Chapter 11):

> In schools, those under instruction are too customarily looked upon as acquiring knowledge as theoretical spectators, minds which appropriate knowledge by direct energy of intellect. The very word pupil has almost come to mean one who is engaged not in having fruitful experiences but in absorbing knowledge directly. Something which is called mind or consciousness is severed from the physical organs of activity. The former is then thought to be purely intellectual and cognitive; the latter to be an irrelevant and intruding physical factor. The intimate union of activity and undergoing its consequences which leads to recognition of meaning is broken; instead we have two fragments: mere bodily action on one side, and meaning directly grasped by "spiritual" activity on the other.

# DOUBLE-LOOP LEARNING

Drawing heavily from the work of John Dewey, Chris Argyris and Donald Schön (Argyris 1992; Argyris 1993; Argyris and Schön 1996) also contributed tremendously to elevating the dialogue on individual and organizational learning from a discussion of mere skill development to an emphasis on abstract reasoning and critical self-reflection. They noticed that a "disconnect" often existed between an individual's espoused theory of why he did something, and his actual theory-in-action. They suggested that individuals should develop the skill of "reflection in action," a form of thinking that allows one to critically analyze one's own thought processes at varying levels. This form of critical self-reflection, termed double-loop learning, involves reflection on one's own basic assumptions as they arise within the action context. When accomplished successfully, this form of learning can dramatically alter behavior by causing a shift in the core assumptions underlying the way in which problematic situations are perceived.

Verna Allee (1997; 2003) saw double-loop learning as the form of learning that distinguishes what she termed procedural from functional knowledge. While procedural learning is characterized by linear, trial-and-error logic on a predetermined path of action (p. 122), functional knowledge in today's knowledge-intensive organization increasingly requires "evaluation and modification of the goal or objective, as well as design of the path or procedures used to get there." (p. 134)

Allee's description of functional knowledge appears to form a bridge between traditional managerial control of work processes and the pre-specified, non-reflective form of learning characteristic of procedural knowledge. Her description of functional knowledge also implies a degree of systems thinking ability. To actively engage in the critical evaluation of one's goals and objectives, as well as procedures for reaching them, the individual must be aware and act within the constraints of the larger strategic objectives and processes of the organizational system within which his/her actions take place.

The ability to think systemically now becomes more central to knowledge work. Peter Senge (1990; 1994; 1999), for example, attempted to move beyond a focus on individual skill development to view learning at the organizational level. Senge advocated the development of five basic competencies that were designed to foster organizational learning: team learning, personal mastery, mental modeling, shared vision, and systems thinking. While much of the current discussion on essential worker competencies centers on the development of specific skills, Senge began to elevate this discussion to a focus on forms and levels of thinking and how these relate to an organization's strategic initiatives. Stated simply, this amounted to a shift away from a focus on specific knowledge content to the form this knowledge takes within a larger system.

The critical self-reflection entailed in double-loop learning implies the exercise of systems thinking within an action context composed of numerous, dynamic and interdependent dimensions. One dimension involves reflection on one's own thought processes understood as a system occurring within, for example, a functional work group. A broader dimension of reflection entails the wider context of the organization within which increasingly cross-functional work takes place. The organization as action context again must be viewed as a system formulating its strategies within still a larger environment of social, economic and political forces characteristic of the world economy. According to this framework, authority is derived from one's ability to apprehend, articulate and respond to these dimensions and their interrelationships, rather than through the consolidation of knowledge and power. (LaRue 1999; 2002)

While each dimension outlined here indicates levels of reflection and spheres of concern, formulation of individual action occurs on the basis of internalized, normally tacit, theories of how these multiple dimensions interact (Nonaka and Takeuchi 1995; McMaster 1996; Allee 1997; Nonaka and Nishiguchi 2001; Allee 2003; Takeuchi and Nonaka 2004). Because each of these interdependent dimensions is today undergoing constant and accelerating change, it follows that our apprehension of these systems must undergo constant revision. Understood in this way, apprehension of theory at multiple levels and dimensions takes on dramatically heightened importance in the life of the knowledge worker and, by extension, the organization and society as a whole.

Perhaps the words of W. Edwards Deming did not fall on deaf ears when he said: "Without theory, one has no questions to ask. Hence, without theory, there is no learning" (Meril, Covey et al. 1994). Theory, once considered the exclusive purview of the academy and often disdained as irrelevant by much of the business community, now becomes central to the non-routine, dynamic practice characteristic of today's high-flex organization.

Argyris and Schön recognized that certain organizational contexts were more conducive to double-loop learning. They described two organization learning climates which they labeled Model I and Model II organizations. Model I organizations were characterized by unilateral control, win-lose thinking, defensive behavior and secrecy. Model II organizations, by contrast, fostered a climate of openness to inquiry and mutual trust. The Model I organization appears increasingly antithetical to the flexible network firm characterized by rapid change, the imperatives of cross-functionality and the powerful centrifugal force of information and communication technologies. Should a Model I strategy be attempted in such an environment, a competitor organizing according to Model II principles, while fully utilizing the emerging information and communication technologies as tools for the open generation and dissemination of knowledge, would be a formidable and qualitatively new form of opponent.

# HOW THEORY AND ACTION INFORM ONE ANOTHER IN PRACTICE

Two kinds of theory play a crucial role in the Action-Learning process, leading to more effective individual and organizational performance. The first explicit or canonical theory is the one most familiar to academics. It is the theory embodied in books, journal articles, models, and methodologies. McMaster (1996) provides a lucid "operational definition" of the explicit form of theory as "a group of statements, taken as a related whole, that is used as our basis for design, judgment, and guidance of action" (p. 19). This definition of theory, as it is applied to organizational life, is probably quite recognizable to practitioners in the empirical sciences. It is explicit, open to scrutiny, constantly tested against results it can provide, and open to modification.

The second kind is what may be termed tacit or implicit theory. This form is embodied in our unconscious assumptions, silently but powerfully shaping our perspectives and actions (Nonaka and Nishiguchi 2001; Takeuchi and Nonaka 2004). It is so all-pervasive that it becomes illusive and, as such, highly resistant to change.

# THE ROLE OF EXPLICIT THEORY

In Action-Learning seminars we have led in the past (LaRue and Sobol 2002), participants were exposed to a wide range of explicit theoretical knowledge and were required to evaluate explicit theories and test the relevance of what they read through direct application. Participants developed workshops, seminars, and pilot programs in their respective departments to address specific organizational issues. While it was the direct application of explicit theory that led to tangible changes in their organization, we would argue that it was an awareness of the role of tacit or implicit theory in individual and organizational life that had the greatest impact on participants in this program.

# THE ROLE OF IMPLICIT THEORY

In his further discussion of the role of theory in organizational life, McMaster (1996, p. 19) writes, "In corporations, people are unconscious of theory because it is obscured by explicit systems, by control mechanisms, and by accepted management platitudes." He states further that this definition of theory "extends beyond specifics and includes many loosely and tentatively formulated statements as well as any assumptions that underlie the theory—often beyond awareness." (p. 20)

Thus, the realm of implicit theory is tremendously powerful in that it exists, in whole or in part, just below the threshold of our conscious awareness and, as such, is highly resistant to traditional methods of organizational change. One participant, a senior executive in a national wireless telecommunications company, demonstrated his newfound appreciation for the role of implicit theory when he wrote the following in our seminar forum:

> This last year, our company launched three major new services that are part of the strategic plan to create revenue and sustain market share. Two of the three projects were delayed beyond their desired launch dates, and all three experienced adverse customer service reaction.

> When I was in the U.S. Air Force, I was required to drive a 5-ton truck with a transmission that required "double clutching" to shift without clashing or "grinding" the gears. Until that skill was acquired, the gears would grind, the truck lost momentum, and I was left with very few good choices on how to keep going without damaging the vehicle. I see some parallels here with our product/service launches this last year.

> The struggle to enhance our service offerings is not due to lack of skill, dedication, or willingness to work with others. That is demonstrated in the supreme efforts—albeit frantic ones—to launch and support the products/services by members of all company departments. While follow-up meetings have been held to determine what worked and what didn't, we still seem to struggle. It appears there is something more basic and overarching at work here—something so pervasive that it undermines tremendous effort to succeed.

All parts of the organization that are engaged in launching and supporting products/services seem to be motivated by different objectives or theories...The three organizational entities that produce and sustain our products/services should ideally be linked in theory to the timely, cost-effective, and reliable deployment of what we sell. Yet past results seem to show a single-mindedness of each entity towards mostly one part: Product Development is motivated by "time to market," i.e., being the first to market in order to maintain preeminence among the competition. Engineering seems to focus on supporting the Product Development drive for timeliness but with strong focus on cost of development. Operations seem engaged in implementing and maintaining the service with most attention to reliability, i.e., the end customer experience. All three motivations are valid, yet the heavy emphasis by each team often sets up conflicting actions that, in the end, result in diminished project success. (LaRue and Sobol 2002)

These statements clearly demonstrate a renewed capacity to see the organization less in terms of discrete functional roles and more in terms of how these functions—each operating according to their own "theory" of the business—interact. We have found that true and lasting change does not occur unless and until individuals and groups can clearly identify the tacit theories that govern their actions, and are willing to adjust these theories as circumstances warrant.

This form of critical self-reflection at the level of implicit theory is therefore an essential competency of knowledge work and the process of Action-Learning. Often, small shifts in an organization's implicit theories can have a major impact in creating sustainable change. Action-Learning Teams must therefore develop a keen sense of how implicit theory shapes and molds organizational reality. Further, Action-Learning Teams must develop the capability of surfacing implicit theory, testing its relevance against the strategic direction of the organization, and when necessary, making adjustments to these theories in a manner that can be accepted by those inside the organization.

## ORGANIZATIONS AS COMPLEX ADAPTIVE SYSTEMS

The emerging field of Complexity Science has seriously challenged our twentieth-century belief that systems could be understood by reducing them to their constituent parts. Biological systems at every observable level appear to behave in a purposeful manner according to emergent properties that cannot be understood at the level of their individual components. A form of self-organization occurs through seemingly random variation, connections among internal components, and interaction of the organism with its environment to create novel adaptations that cannot be predicted or predetermined in advance.

Applying these principles to human organization is a bit trickier, in that humans have a unique ability to evolve largely independent of biological processes. In short, through our extensions of language, culture, and technology, humans learn, adapt, and evolve in ways that far surpass the speed and sophistication of other biological forms. Said another way, humans not only adapt to their environment, but also increasingly *adapt their environment to themselves.* This capacity has had far-reaching and often unforeseen consequences that are unparalleled elsewhere in nature. For example, the emergence of global information and communication networks represent a literal *extension* of the human nervous system. We simply have no known historical precedent or biological equivalent of this form of evolution, nor have we fully reckoned with its implications.

As has been noted in various ways throughout this book, our strength as humans to alter our environment is also potentially our weakness. That is, we tend to operate according to largely unconscious assumptions that frame our world and our interaction with our environment. These assumptions are a foundational code of operations much like the invisible core programming of a computer is a platform for the use of all other software and peripheral hardware.

## COMPLEXITY AND SPIRAL DYNAMICS

Spiral Dynamics (Beck and Cowan 1995) offers one potentially powerful explanatory framework for human evolution independent of the biological processes mentioned earlier. Based upon the work of the late Dr. Clare Graves, Spiral Dynamics illustrates an invisible evolutionary code of operations in human beings as follows:

1. Genetic DNA is biological code for physical human evolution.
2. Cultural 'DNA' is a bio-psycho-social code for human evolution composed of the myriad of influences that make up our value systems on the individual, organizational, and societal levels.

Both forms of human DNA are comprised of specific systemic traits that are both identifiable and uniquely balanced within every individual. The cultural DNA frame of reference is so intrinsic to human 'being', that it is often invisible to the conscious mind (like the core programming of a computer is invisible to the user) and, thus, highly resistant to change. However, like biological genetics, human bio-psycho-social systems (known as memetic systems of core values) can, and do evolve both up and down the evolutionary spiral when life conditions signal a change is necessary.

Some of the seminal research in the area of Complexity Science emerged from the work of The Santa Fe Institute. Influential authors here include (Waldrop 1992; Kauffman 1995). The

London School of Economics (Mitleton-Kelly 2001) is also conducting research into the application of Complexity Science to the field of organization change. A number of authors are also exploring the application of Complexity Science to knowledge management, including the processes of knowledge creation and transfer (Stacey 2003; Stacey and Griffin 2005; Tsoukas 2005) Other authors who are making contributions to this field as it relates broadly to human organization include (Tsoukas 1994; Hock 1999; Gould 2000; Hock 2000; Johnson 2001; Wilber 2001; Capra 2002; Tsoukas, Knudsen et al. 2003; Tsoukas and Mylonopoulos 2004; Tsoukas and Shepherd 2004; Tsoukas 2005).

While relatively little is understood about the application of the emerging science of Complexity to the human sphere, what we learn in the years ahead will most certainly have a profound effect on organization theory and the field of Action-Learning as we know it today.

# PART III

# SUPPLEMENTAL MATERIALS

In the following section, we will examine how the U.S. Army used Action-Learning Team concepts to transform their culture. We will also examine a case study of one of our Action-Learning Team processes used to develop leadership competencies in a large, technologically complex organization. We will also explore how to use the principles of Action-Learning within a networked learning environment for the development of distributed Action-Learning Teams.

# 11 THE TRANSFORMATION OF THE U.S. ARMY THROUGH ACTION-LEARNING TEAMS

*Special contribution by*
*Major General Robert R. Ivany*

## ACTION-LEARNING TEAMS IN THE U.S. ARMY

Probably the least likely organization in which we would expect to find vigorous Action-Learning Teams is the United States Army. The army, like most military institutions, has the reputation of being conservative, hierarchical, and bound by centuries of tradition. Yet some of the most impressive recent cultural and operational changes have come from the uniformed ranks. The stunning victories of Desert Storm, the occupation of Bosnia and Kosovo, the overthrow of the Taliban in Afghanistan and the lightning push to Baghdad in 2003 captured the interest, if not the admiration, of the entire world.

How did they do it? How did an organization, regarded as ponderous, reluctant to change and wedded to "doing things the army way" become synonymous with "speed, adaptability and flexibility?" Significant national investment in people and resources was essential, but the one key aspect that observers often overlook is a transformation within the organization. This transformation was brought about by a major change in the way the army conducted its business – in short, its organizational culture. As you have seen in Chapter 2 on Inquiry, (Figure 3), changing an organization's culture cascades transformation throughout an organization, whether it is the army or any other enterprise.

The Mojave Desert, with 115 degree temperatures, searing sun and biting sand, was the unlikely birthplace of this transformation. Beginning in the early 1980s, units were rotated through an expansive exercise area known as the National Training Center where, with the help of sophisticated laser technology, cameras, a highly trained opposing force unit and an elite group of observer/controllers (or O/Cs), the revolution began in earnest. No longer could military leaders play war games and argue about which tank fired first in mock battles. The technology and the ever-present team of O/Cs exposed excuses and cut short disputes between opposing forces. It quickly became apparent that leaders relying on elaborate operational plans had to become far more flexible in the face of a smart opposing force that delighted in doing the unexpected. Leaders at all levels who were committed to "fighting the plan" instead of allowing subordinates to make timely decisions to move combat units, shift artillery concentrations, or reroute logistical routes, suffered embarrassing defeats.

The losses on the battlefields could not, in and of themselves, bring about the behavioral and operational changes that leaders realized were necessary to win these realistic and demanding battles.

# THE EMERGENCE OF THE AFTER ACTION REVIEW (AAR)

What was needed was an effective process to translate the lessons learned into immediate changes in tactics and, at the same time, sow the seeds for a far-ranging change within the army itself. As a result, the army's own unique Action-Learning process emerged in the form of the After Action Review (or AAR). It was a simple, inexpensive but brutally honest way to discover what really happened in an engagement, why it happened and how the unit could sustain its strong capabilities and improve its weak ones. The AAR not only exposed the failings of a plan, but cast a spotlight on reluctant leaders who failed to make timely decisions based on what Clauswitz, the famous military thinker, called "the friction and fog of war," or what Peter Drucker called "the exploitation of unforeseen opportunities." How did the AAR help bring about this operational and cultural change?

It was a straightforward, revealing, and simple procedure. After each operation, the leaders of the unit and its members reviewed what the objectives of the operation were, what actually happened, what went well and what did not. These reviews differed substantially from the critiques of the past. A facilitator, in these cases the O/C, ran the review. Senior leaders learned to listen, take notes and speak only when asked to answer questions or clarify their guidance. The facilitator was interested in only three points:

What was the unit's mission?
What actually happened?
What were the three capabilities the unit must sustain and three it must improve?

That was it.

# LEADERS WHO LEARN FROM THEIR SUBORDINATES

Discovering the answers to these questions required soldiers at every level to contribute without fear of retribution or concern for the bruised egos of their superiors. The O/Cs relentlessly sought the root causes of events. It was not enough to learn what went wrong or right. Why did it happen? Was it a faulty plan? Poor training? Lack of communication? With each level of probing, more and more of the inner capabilities of the unit were exposed and examined. It became apparent that not only were trust and honesty essential for a fruitful AAR, but they were indispensable for a vastly empowered organization.

A scared soldier worried about a reprimand for failing to accomplish her assigned task was not likely to stand up and draw attention to her failure. A junior leader whose superior failed to give him adequate preparation time had to be confident that he would not lose face or any other part of his anatomy if he pointed this out. Slowly but surely, leaders at all levels grew tough skins and learned to accept public notice of their shortcomings. When leaders gracefully accepted responsibility and blame, the rest of the unit gladly followed suit.

Only thinking soldiers, flexible plans and, above all, timely decisions emerged victorious. In order to win the wars of the future, the army had to change not only the way it fought its battles, but the relationship between ranks, the openness of its hierarchy and its receptiveness to recommendations from all levels. In order to win, colonels learned from privates. In order to develop a flexible mind-set and anticipatory thinking, the generals' responsibility shifted from making all the decisions to "setting the conditions" for others to respond to, or better yet, to anticipate the shifting battlefield. The organization which waited for orders from headquarters found itself defeated time and again.

These drastic changes took foreign visitors by surprise. Many left the National Training Center shaking their heads with astonishment. "Our senior leaders would never allow such honest and open reviews by their peers and subordinates," they lamented. "This sort of thing is not done in our country."

In the U.S., however, the impact of the AAR spread through every unit in the army. Soon every operation from parades to picnics included AARs. They created empathy through mutual understanding of what occurred in highly- complex operations.

Everyone could air grievances or make recommendations during the review.

## ACHIEVING SYNERGY THROUGH CROSS-FUNCTIONAL ALIGNMENT

As issues were discussed openly and freely, leaders gained a deeper appreciation of each other's capabilities. The importance of standards, ethics and shared values was constantly discussed. The engineer learned about the limitations of the infantryman who better understands the contributions of the logistician or the insights of the communications specialist.

The army realized that combat teams composed of many specialists, the army's version of Action-Learning Teams, had to train and work together and, most of all, to trust each other to realize the synergy required to win on the modern battlefield. It was not enough to have the teams on paper. They needed the AAR process to learn together, to harness their collective energies and focus them on identified capabilities. The AAR did more than address collective and individual shortfalls; it prompted even more innovation and feedback.

## FROM AFTER ACTION REVIEW TO LEARNING IN ACTION

Leaders realized that they did not have to wait for an operation to end before conducting an AAR. Rather, at periodic intervals, leaders had mini-AARs to assess the status of an ongoing operation. They then integrated the lessons into the operation to fix problems before they caused failure. It was Action-Learning at its finest. The AAR had evolved from being a historical vehicle to one that could solve issues facing teams in the present.

# ACTION-LEARNING AND KNOWLEDGE MANAGEMENT IN THE ARMY

The effects of the AAR went beyond the immediate exercise. They prompted the introduction of a vastly improved knowledge management system within the army. By taking advantage of information technology, lessons learned could be easily recorded, retrieved and disseminated. The Center for Army Lessons Learned was created to catalogue and distribute these lessons. Commanders could benefit from not only their own AARs but from those of units throughout the army. This system, however beneficial, nonetheless proved to be too slow and cumbersome for junior leaders.

Young commanders wanted to network and discuss operations or exercises in real time! Showing remarkable initiative and eager to find a way to disseminate the lessons even more rapidly among themselves, they established their own Web site, *http://www.companycommander.com*. Here, young captains could exchange the latest information on everything from preparing for deployments overseas to outwitting the opposing forces at the National Training Center. Their knowledge network emphasized the maxim that the authors of this book value so highly: "relevant knowledge in a form they could apply, test and refine in practice." As the AAR process encouraged leaders to learn from their subordinates, *companycommander.com* facilitated peers sharing insights on what worked and what didn't.

# UNDERSTANDING THE LEADER'S INTENT

The desire to build truly integrated, knowledge-based Action-Learning Teams soon spawned yet another initiative. Realizing that fast-moving operations demanded initiative by subordinates, commanders began writing a concise statement explaining the overarching purpose for each operation. Written in his own words and no longer than a short paragraph, the commander provided a "feel" for what he wanted to accomplish.

Providing a "gut feel" for the operation was not something new. During World War II, truly good orders gave similar guidance to subordinates. Consider the feel of the order that the Combined Planning Staff gave General Dwight D. Eisenhower before the invasion of Normandy: "Enter the continent of Europe and, in conjunction with other Allied Nations, undertake operations aimed at the heart of Germany and the destruction of her armed forces." These were vigorous, empowering but concise words that perfectly described what was expected without explaining the "how" of the numerous campaigns that would be fought and won.

In the absence of specific orders, each subordinate leader was expected to act in accord with the overall purpose or "commander's intent" of the operation. Initiative was encouraged; waiting for orders was not. Soon, "Commander's Intent" statements were required in every order. They became readily accepted as clear, concise statements of what a team must do to succeed with respect to the opposition. Senior leaders began to issue operational plans that gave maximum freedom of action to subordinates and reserved for themselves only the most critical decisions.

# THE EMERGENCE OF THE "VUCA" WORLD

The transformation came just in time. If the national security environment was dangerous in the 1980s, it became even more volatile in the decades that followed. In fact, the Army War College developed an acronym to describe the drastically changed situation: VUCA became a widely recognized term. It stood for Volatile, Uncertain, Complex and Ambiguous.

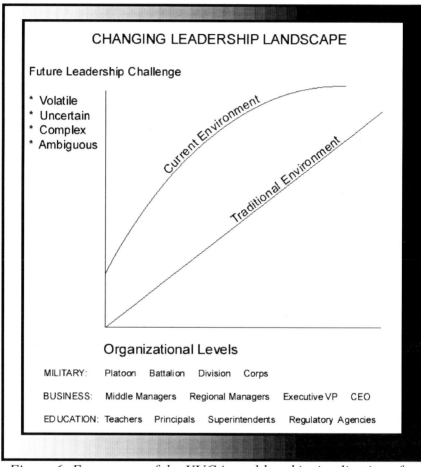

*Figure 6: Emergence of the VUCA world and its implications for modern military, business, and education.*

It aptly described the new world of terrorism, biochemical warfare, narco-traffic and a persistent danger to the American homeland. VUCA, of course, had always existed. Generals, corporate presidents and government officials operated in a VUCA world. The higher in an organization a leader reached, the more of a VUCA environment she operated in. What changed was that now junior leaders found themselves in volatile, uncertain, complex, and ambiguous environments. Without definitive orders for every situation, they suddenly had to make critical decisions on issues previously reserved for much more senior leaders. Furthermore, they could expect scrutiny by a host of non-governmental organizations and the international media.

Now the action of a young lieutenant whose soldiers guarded a key bridge in Bosnia could be debated by everyone from the U.N. High Commissioner to representatives of Doctors Without Borders. The introduction of high-speed communications meanwhile allowed international news organizations to comment within hours on the ability of a sergeant in the Special Forces to direct laser-guided missiles on a suspected Taliban fighting position.

No picture better captured the modern VUCA world than the highly-publicized photograph of Special Forces troops riding small ponies into battle with their Northern Alliance tribal allies in 2001 shortly after the terrorist attack on America. What captured the imagination of Americans was the unlikely scene of soldiers on horseback in the 21st century. The truly remarkable aspect, however, was that these Action-Learning Teams of 13 Special Forces which were made up of military personnel from the Army, Navy, Air Force and Marines had literally dropped out of the sky, linked up with Uzbek tribesmen and persuaded them to ride into battle against a far better armed and numerous Taliban. These Americans dropped aerial bombs on the enemy and then coordinated a swift occupation of the entire Afghan countryside.

*Figure 7: Special Forces teams riding into battle on horseback in Afghanistan. Photo used with permission of the U.S. Army.*

No training manual could have prepared these elite troops for the challenges they faced. Their two- to three-year training and education programs had not only taught them how to use satellite computers, global positioning systems and laser designators, but it stressed their ability to think through unforeseen developments and hidden opportunities. They learned how to think, not what to do. It was these captains, not colonels, who made the difference on the ground. They moved rapidly, showed remarkable adaptability and displayed quiet courage as they and their horse-borne allies toppled the Taliban and achieved a remarkable victory in only 39 days. Suddenly, the world realized that there was more than technology to the transformation of America's armed forces.

The cultural transformation that began in the Mojave Desert 20 years earlier had borne fruit. Open communication between ranks and organizations, the receptivity to constant improvement, and the emphasis on acting in accord with the commander's intent became the hallmark of a vastly different fighting force.

The simple AAR based on trust and honesty initiated changes never envisioned by its founders. Military leaders found a vehicle that allowed them to focus their energies and encourage continued innovation. If a traditional, conservative organization such as the United States Army can develop its version of Action-Learning Teams, every modern organization can do the same.

# APPLYING LESSONS LEARNED FROM THE AAR

Action-Learning can become the catalyst for change in any organization, and it requires few resources. Facilitators from within the organization who are not directly involved in a program make excellent facilitators.  Often, company veterans who have spent their time in administrative positions are delighted to take on this role and become involved in day-to-day business operations.

As soon as the "boss" participates in an AAR and allows the facilitator some running room, openly taking responsibility and blame, a positive change in culture follows almost immediately. As soon as employees speak up and provide previously hidden insights, the organization will improve and develop useful networks.

Web sites are the fastest and most economical way for a corporation to share knowledge across boundaries. If required, they can be password-protected with limited access, keeping in mind that the wider the access, the better the opportunity to harvest insights and knowledge. Simple Web sites with minimum structure work best; *companycommander.com* is a superb example.

Just as army leaders innovated on the original AAR concept with mini-AARs, so too can corporations of any size modify their AAR to create a synergy within their Action-Learning Teams.  Many organizations use the AAR as a tool for mentoring and coaching, taking advantage of lessons learned to help members of the organization grow. As long as participants are confident that they will not suffer as a result of their honesty, they will continue to participate and take ownership of future programs.

Leaders who have the courage to listen to their team members while respecting their shortcomings can develop a valuable Action-Learning Team. They will reap the benefits of increased productivity and improved retention for a very modest investment.

Trust and honesty are, after all, free.

# ABOUT BOB IVANY

Bob Ivany has presided over one of the nation's most respected institutions for the education of strategic leaders: the U.S. Army War College. There, for three years, he instituted programs to develop the next generation of military and civilian leaders from the U.S. and 42 other countries to meet the challenges of cultural change, organizational transformation, and a drastically altered national security environment.

Prior to leading the Army War College, General Ivany assisted several countries in the transformation and democratization of their military forces, including Saudi Arabia and Kuwait following Desert Storm. Throughout these distinguished engagements, General Ivany has made extensive use of Action-Learning Teams using the After Action Review approach and has first-hand experience of the cultural transformation it has produced throughout the army.

# 12 EXECUTIVE MASTERY - CYBERSPACE AND THE NEW FRONTIERS OF EXECUTIVE EDUCATION

## A CASE STUDY IN ONLINE ACTION-LEARNING

By Bruce LaRue and Mark R. Sobol
*This chapter was reprinted with permission from (LaRue and Sobol 2002)*

## IT BEGAN AS FACE-TO-FACE COACHING

During the spring of 2000, we were engaged to provide coaching for several executives within the engineering division of a leading telecommunications provider responsible for the design, implementation, and operation of its national cellular network. John, a recently promoted vice president, led the team. He was a longtime veteran of the telecommunications business, an "old hand" whose vast experience and maturity could help to temper the relative youth of his peers. John was at the same time on the glide path to retirement in just four years and eagerly looked forward to the day when he could put his career behind him. From his perspective, the pace of change and the complexity of today's business environment seemed better suited to younger leaders.

The prime operating characteristic of the team was that it acted as a collection of "silos," working independently of each other except during their obligatory monthly management meeting, where discourse was generally limited to reports from the six functional areas. Rarely could the team members ever be said to "think together." During a coaching session, we began to explore ways to provide developmental support to the members of John's management team, in keeping with his stated goal of "building the bench strength" of his organization during this time of great change and growth. He set as his measurement of success "the number of managers deemed ready for promotion" by the end of the year. We suggested adopting the combination of an online and face-to-face coaching and education model to meet the challenge.

# EVOLUTION TO ONLINE COACHING, EDUCATION, AND ORGANIZATIONAL DEVELOPMENT

We began with a team meeting followed by two rounds of individual interviews for gauging interest and establishing the "What's in it for me?" factor. John made it clear to all, however, that there was no requirement to participate. Together with the team, we determined that there was sufficient interest and desire to move ahead. It was evident that there was no small amount of trepidation about the increased workload, which added several additional hours to an already demanding schedule in a 7-day-a-week, 24-hour-a-day operation. So, with a mixture of curiosity, excitement, and fear, we commenced a 12-week observation and dialogue to explore organizational systems from three interrelated dimensions: the individual, the organization, and society. As our face-to-face and online dialogue progressed, a clear image of the current state of the team began to emerge for all to observe from a variety of different perspectives.

This exploration was meant to enable the participants to discern the assumptions (Drucker, 1999, p. 182) and implicit theories (McMaster, 1996) permeating their organization. It was also designed to surface their espoused theories and "theories-in-use" (Argyris, 1978, 1990, 1992, 1993; Argyris & Schön, 1996) by gaining a deeper appreciation for the gap between these two poles of understanding. When their tacit knowledge became explicit (Nonaka & Takeuchi, 1995) for all to hear, the foundation for preparing the leaders to design and implement their own organizational development initiatives was created with minimal reliance on external resources. As we will see, our intention to build *internal capacity* for organizational change in John's director team (rather than perpetuating a traditional form of dependence on external consultants) proved to be a crucial theme of the learning initiative.

What we were unable to predict, however, was that this training would quickly lead to personal and organizational transformation through what came to be known as the Executive MasterClass™ Program. As the participants began to compare and contrast the current state of their team and organization with different theories of operation, a new awareness emerged. The participants reported a heightened sense of consciousness of themselves, their teammates, and their organization. A reflective dialogue was sparked during the 12-week learning process in which the team explored a variety of ways in which to make changes to their personal, team, and organizational behavior.

In the sections that follow, we outline the manner in which we structured the online learning program around the unique needs and challenges that John and his team faced. Along the way, we outline the core principles that serve as the foundation of the Executive MasterClass™ Program together with their broader implications for executive education in the 21st century.

# STRUCTURING THE INTERVENTION, CONNECTING WITH THE TEAM

We first met with John to determine his team's learning and development goals. We wanted to get a sense of his long-term learning objectives while gaining a deeper understanding of the more immediate issues for which he was seeking resolution. Although John had his own goals in mind for his team, the team members were encouraged to determine what was in it for them. The learning opportunity we developed needed to be in alignment with both personal career objectives and the organization's business strategy. Paradoxically, this meant that the learning system we constructed would contribute to making each participant more marketable outside the firm.

Although this approach extends the goals of the learning process beyond those of the current organization, we have found that this is an essential component of an overall retention strategy. Any effective learning system must be sensitive to both the unique learning needs of each individual *and* the organization. We believe that if the learning and development needs of knowledge workers are continually met, they will find little need to venture outside the walls of the firm.

Based on our interviews with John's team members, we knew that we had to construct this learning opportunity in a way that was sensitive to and integrated with their already demanding personal and professional lives. They were familiar with traditional classroom approaches to learning, but they generally found these approaches to be quite disruptive and irrelevant to their personal and work lives. They also found these traditional approaches to lack the kind of stimulating interaction among their peers that they desired. The same held true for many Web-based systems, such as computer-based training, that focus on content delivery rather than peer interaction.

In essence, the aim of this learning initiative was to develop effective communities of practice that were focused on the creation and application of new knowledge rather than to deliver a certain content of knowledge from teacher to student. (For more on the principle of communities of practice, see, e.g., (Lave and Wenger 1991; Lesser 2000; Lesser, Fontaine et al. 2000; Brown and Duguid 2002)

We also understood that we were dealing with highly skilled and accomplished specialists in their respective fields of endeavor. Therefore, the aim of this proposed learning system was not to further this area of specialized technical knowledge but rather to develop competencies in and gain a deeper understanding of the areas *of organizational development, change,* and *personal mastery.*

By the term *personal mastery,* we refer to the ability of the participants to stand outside of their current situations and their own limited perspectives. This allows the managers or executives to obtain a level of distance from their current challenges and to see them from the broader context of interdependent relationships, political forces, and environmental and market changes and to choose the most suitable approach for moving their organization forward. As we will see, the online learning component of this program played a central role in the development of personal mastery.

# THE ONLINE SYSTEM

John's director team happened to be co-located, while many of the sub-organizations reporting to his directors were distributed across the country. Like many modern organizations, his team members needed to build competence in managing distributed work teams. For this reason, and because of their extremely busy and varied schedules, we decided to conduct the program with a mixture of face-to-face and online work. The online system we used was a

Web-based asynchronous groupware system, allowing the team members to conduct their work from anywhere in the world and at any time convenient for them within the agreed-on pace and structure of the program. The asynchronous nature of the system allowed the learning experience to occur with a minimum of disruption to the normal workflow of the team members, while at the same time capturing and organizing their knowledge in one central location.

## CASTING THE NET

We also learned that John and his directors rarely met to work together aside from monthly strategy meetings, unless an emergency or other contingency compelled them to do so. To stimulate greater interaction among the entire team, we divided the members into groups of approximately three members each. These became known as *lead* teams. Each lead team was assigned a leadership role in consecutive two-week sections of the 12-week learning module and was responsible for generating a reflective commentary on assigned reading materials. After posting responses to designated areas in the groupware system, the rest of the group provided critical commentary on the work of the lead team with a specific eye toward the development of new applications.

Each of the lead teams was responsible for generating a reflective commentary on assigned reading materials, with an emphasis on the implications of what its members had read for their organizational practice. Following the regular postings to designated areas in the groupware system, the rest of the group provided critical commentary on the work of the lead team, again with a specific eye toward suggesting further areas for application to their workplace.

# COMBINING FACE-TO-FACE MEETINGS WITH WEB-BASED LEARNING - THE ONE-DAY ORIENTATION RETREAT

We began the program with a one-day orientation retreat in which we provided participants with a highly focused orientation to the Executive MasterClass™ Program, the online groupware system, and basic norms of online collaborative learning. On the surface, norms of online discourse might seem self-evident. They are essential to creating a safe and productive learning environment. Because the online environment lacks many of the normal physical cues present in face-to-face dialogue, it is essential to make one's emotional intent clear through writing. We also emphasized the importance of timely interaction so as to keep pace with the agreed-on structure and timing of the course.

Because participants are required to provide feedback to one another's work, we stressed the importance of (a) being timely, (b) being constructive, (c) paraphrasing and asking clarifying questions rather than assuming the intent of the writer, (d) differentiating between critical commentary and criticism, and (e) offering suggestions rather than merely pointing out problems. We suggested these basic norms, and participants modified them and developed others based on personal and group preferences.

# MONTHLY FACE-TO-FACE MEETINGS

We met off-site once a month, where we spent approximately six hours with John and his team members. The time was used to engage in further dialogue around pressing concerns facing their organization *in light of what they had learned*. As we will see in later sections of this chapter, through the structured use of online dialogue, we were able to continue uninterrupted our exploration of the critical issues begun in these meetings. In this way, we were able to build and sustain a level of momentum and exploration not possible in face-to-face meetings alone. We now provide a sample of the kind of dialogue we engaged in to raise the level of awareness of John's team, followed by a discussion of the critical role of online discourse in this process.

# BLENDING THEORY AND PRACTICE

We took John's team members through various group exercises designed to surface conflicting organizational theories operating in their organization and to develop ideas for resolving conflicts. We wove the discussion into the theoretical themes explored in the course by providing a bridge between the normally obtuse realm of theory and the thorny problems of daily work.

We drew connections between their tacit understanding of work and how their assumptions live through their actions. For example, we queried the following:

> "Are organizations machines and the people within them mindless cogs in need of strict control, or are they interdependent elements of a highly intelligent organism in need of inspiration and challenge in order to move them into higher levels of achievement and personal mastery?" "Do the assumptions living in your organization have anything at all to do with the precipitous decline in morale you are witnessing and to your ability to attract and retain top talent?" "How are declines in morale and loss of talent affecting your bottom line, especially when this talent often leaves only to enrich the coffers of your competition?"

The history of the Industrial Age, we suggested, appeared to be strongly associated with the systematic elimination of the human factor from the production equation. This is the legacy of Frederick Taylor and his many reincarnations through total quality management and various forms of statistical process control, lean manufacturing, just-in-time manufacturing, reengineering, and nine-tenths of the management fads of the month. Mechanical and information-based automation seemed to support the acceleration toward de-skilled work while, paradoxically, emerging forces in the economy demanded increased levels of knowledge and competence from workers. "If your workers were truly valued as assets and legitimate stakeholders in your company, then why are they still relegated to the cost side of your accounting ledger?" "How is Taylor's legacy affecting your management decisions to this day," we asked, "and how does this behavior stand up in light of Drucker's (1999; 2002) assertion that today's knowledge workers must be treated like volunteers – their commitment earned, not assumed?" The room would often fall silent.

During our frequent breaks, the halls hummed with cell phone conversations and the click of laptop keyboards as directors clambered to return scores of messages accumulated during the previous hour. We heard mutterings of Taylor, Drucker, HBR, Xerox PARC, and Nonaka. But would this buzz of dialogue evaporate as we emerged from this elegant boardroom? On the contrary, our questions stimulated discussion that would flourish in the halls of our virtual learning environment over the coming weeks.

Many readers of this chapter have undoubtedly experienced countless weekend conferences and workshops where condensed exercises in workplace enlightenment are explored, only to find newfound enthusiasm and understanding evaporate in the glaring light of the Monday morning grind. Some readers might even have naively imagined themselves sharing their insights with eager colleagues, only to find that the colleagues' eagerness to meet with them had more to do with project deadlines they had overlooked or new crises that had emerged in their absence. Normalcy soon sets in, relegating the insights of the previous weekend to that of a quaint, but now largely irrelevant, respite from real life. If anything, the weekend foray generates jealousy rather than interest back at work.

# MEANWHILE, BACK AT THE WEB SITE ... INSIGHTS EMERGE

In the Executive MasterClass™ program, dialogue generated during our monthly meetings moved seamlessly into the online environment. We continually reinforced the integration between relevant literature and the issues that John's team faced. Critical problems were engaged not in the heat of the moment but rather through the thoughtful lenses of all participants, each contributing his or her insights. Unlike phone or e-mail conversations, the participants' thinking is preserved, organized, and easily retrieved.

A critical issue that arose involved new product rollouts. Serious problems routinely surfaced as the deadline for implementation of these new services rapidly approached. Customers were anxiously awaiting the new service based on heavy pre-release marketing initiatives, making delays a matter of serious company-wide concern. As the division of the company responsible for operation and maintenance of the national cellular network, John's team felt an inordinate share of the responsibility for ensuring the reliability of the new service. Yet it was also the last division in the functional food chain to engage in the process of developing and implementing the new initiative. The team had little input into the timing of its release or in the development of the engineering infrastructure for its operation. These crucial responsibilities were the domains of marketing and engineering, two separate and distinct functional silos concerned almost exclusively with their respective roles – often to the detriment of the broader process.

As one might imagine, no small amount of heated finger-pointing and blame ensued as deadlines neared, with John's team feeling most of the heat. From the perspective of each functional division, the blame for problems with the new service offering lay elsewhere. If problems were identified at the functional level, then solutions were expeditiously sought and remedies were put in place, only to see similar problems emerge with the next new product rollout. In some respects, it appeared that, as each division became more efficient, problems between divisions intensified. The result was often a less than desirable customer experience, loss of market share, and rapidly declining morale across the organization.

Why, after intensely focusing precious time, resources, and talent, were these problems seeming to intensify rather than go away? Would more of the same management methods achieve a different result, or was an entirely new tack necessary? If the latter, then what would this new approach look like? Should we create a task force, convene a committee, or hire a team of consultants to "fix" the problem? Or perhaps yet another reorganization was in order. His colleagues wholeheartedly affirmed him when Richard, one of John's directors, wrote in our virtual dialogue forum that it might be time to reconsider this approach as well:

> It seems like "reorganization" has become commonplace in our vocabulary. Some of the reading material suggests that we need to throw away the standard solutions and responses we've always used in the past to deal with change. Is our problem that we're still trying to find the right organizational structure or fit to deal with the competitive challenges we face? Are we in the mode of using reorganization as our standard answer when we discover something isn't working or we're not meeting stated goals? Is it possible that some groups still haven't caught up with the last reorganization and are now even further out of sync with the rest of the organization?

It is relevant for the purposes of this chapter to point out that Richard was a very thoughtful yet reserved individual. In regular face-to-face staff meetings, many of which we attended, Richard was usually the last to speak, and when he did so, his reserved demeanor often left his valuable contributions vulnerable to being overshadowed by more vocal members of John's team. In fact, John had confided in me that although Richard was an extremely talented engineer and trusted manager, this issue had contributed to his being overlooked for promotions in the past.

In the online learning environment, Richard came alive. His thoughtful and articulate reflections and responses to the work of his colleagues were on display. Unlike staff meetings, where others might unwittingly overshadow his voice in the urgency of the moment, Richard's words echo to this day within the virtual walls of our course forum. In the world of online learning, Richard's weakness had suddenly become his strength.

The online learning environment provided a crucial opportunity of pause, continuity, and structured reflection among participants. Although meetings, workshops, task forces, and committees were the order of the day, the online learning environment offered a bridge that allowed the thinking and work of the group, begun in face-to-face meetings, to continue in an organized and coherent manner, largely irrespective of space and time. Participants could compose and reflect on their own thinking in the privacy of their homes, or in airports or hotels, and share it with their colleagues, who would reflect on it yet further. No one interrupts another person; no one has to rearrange his or her schedule; everyone is heard; and new knowledge is created, organized, and stored for future use.

## INSIGHTS LEAD TO ORGANIZATIONAL INTERVENTIONS

As we progressed toward the final third of the learning module, we asked participants to generate specific organizational interventions based on the integration of learning from previous weeks and to focus on a pressing need they faced in and among their respective functional areas. Generating initiatives in coordination with their bosses and peers also made the acceptance and implementation of these initiatives far smoother than previous attempts at change that tended to come down from the top of the organization.

At this point, the power and creativity of the team members was unleashed. The dialogue and learning that they had experienced during the previous weeks provided them with an entirely new perspective and lexicon. Their interactions had given all of them a new level of awareness about themselves, their teammates, and the interrelationships among their organizational units. They no longer perceived their problems in isolation but instead had gained a new sense of perspective as to how the issues with which they struggled were related to the other functional areas of their vast organization. As two directors wrote:

> I have greater awareness of the bigger picture and of the organization. I am beginning to give everything more thought and reflection. I feel a greater personal ownership and optimism. I have come to know this team better.

> A lot has changed for me. I previously had a fairly broad view of things but not very deep. I have expanded my view in both ways. I see myself focused on things I had not been focused on before. I feel more aware. I am refreshed by the differences and perspectives on our team – what we all bring to the table. I have a new appreciation and feeling for all and am feeling connected and more compelled to speak out to influence and make a difference. Now I want to learn how to reach out to other teams.

Based on their heightened sense of awareness and the shared language they had developed together, John's team members engaged in the creation of cross-functional organizational initiatives of which they could share the pride of authorship. Two initiatives were aimed at resolving conflicting organizational theories, and two others were focused on knowledge management and the development of the attributes of a learning organization.

One director, Nick, wrote a proposal that, in his words, was designed to do the following:

> Arouse desire to understand what jewels of learning are already embedded in daily work experience that lead to the power of technical know-how. And then, how to put into practice a few key actions which will further enhance the learning process and the accumulation of technical knowledge.

As we can see from his own comments, Nick had come to realize that his technical organization relied far less on the tangible explicit forms of knowledge embodied in procedure manuals and formal training. Instead, he had come to more fully appreciate the need to capitalize on the informal know-how and improvisation that routinely arise as "these maps and guides fail." Because Nick's proposal was developed in collaboration with his peers and boss, it was immediately accepted and funded. In addition, another director, Richard, integrated many of the learning and knowledge requirements outlined in Nick's proposal in his own initiative focusing on the specifications of an enterprise-wide knowledge management system. Both sets of recommendations, together with those of the entire group, were then used in the development and deployment of this system overseen by another vice president.

In yet another combined effort, three other directors teamed up with John to create a "learning history" Kleiner & Roth (1998) designed to document in detail the problems and successes associated with their most previous product rollout. Using this simple yet highly systematic approach, they were able to demonstrate clearly the recurring problems associated with the introduction of new products and services. Based on this learning history, John in turn was able to express very eloquently one of the most fundamental systemic problems facing their organization as a whole: that there were at least three implicit conflicting theories operating in their organization. As a result, the work of John and his director team was brought to the attention of the leader of the entire company, which in turn has brought about fundamental changes in the manner in which new products are brought to market.

In the sections that follow, we demonstrate how the online component of this learning experience played a pivotal role in surfacing the insights that led to this heightened internal capacity to generate organizational change.

# FORGING A NEW DEVELOPMENTAL PERSPECTIVE - A HIGHER ORDER OF CONSCIOUSNESS

Throughout this entire learning process, program facilitators continually reinforced a sense of the importance of shared responsibility, cross-functional collaboration, and a systems-level perspective among participants. Whereas blame and finger-pointing had been the order of the day as an unrelenting barrage of problems in the organization emerged, John's team had now gained a new sense of shared accountability and responsibility for identifying and correcting the issues underlying these problems. As one director remarked, "If we are not going to make these changes, who is?" They had indeed begun to turn the corner from what Robert Kegan refers to as the "third order" of consciousness into the "fourth order." (Kegan, 1994; see also Kegan & Lahey, 2001)

Characterized by a sense of dependency and the feeling that the power for change lies outside of oneself, Kegan likens the third order of consciousness to the rebelliousness and dependency of the adolescent. This ambivalent, at times even contemptuous, stance toward authority is mirrored in the traditional relationship between the employer and his/her subordinates. By contrast, this learning intervention helped to foster a sense of self-authorship and perspective akin to becoming a mature adult. For example, "I remembered the way I think. This experience is allowing me to feel like an adult in the organization again. This has made life less stressful, I have gained perspective."

Although many employers have gone to great lengths to promote empowerment, self-direction, and personal accountability in their managers and employees, these initiatives may unwittingly strengthen what we see as a silo mentality along the lines of functional and departmental specializations. In turn, these lead to higher levels of fragmentation as organizational units work at cross-purposes rather than with a shared and more systemic view of the whole organization. This silo mentality, and its dysfunctional consequences, could often be traced to deeply held tacit assumptions that were uncovered during this learning process. As one director wrote:

> I have learned that this process has helped me to reevaluate myself and the world around me. I need to find ways to keep doing this. I am more awake. I am excited by the opportunity of challenging myself and working with others. As I have gotten to know the members of this team better, I realize there is so much more there – who people are and their depth of knowledge is eye-opening.

The ability to function as an individual based on an understanding of the system or systems within which one is operating (seeing oneself and the organization from the "outside in") is what Kegan (1994) terms the evolution from an inherently dependent mode of functioning, the third order, to a higher level, the fourth order of consciousness.

Through intense cross-functional dialogue that judiciously combined face-to-face meetings with online discourse, the level of awareness and accountability in John's team had risen markedly. The typical "silver bullet" solution through dependence on external consultants had been replaced with a heightened sense of personal responsibility through facilitated online dialogue.

# LESSONS LEARNED FROM PRAXIS: THE HIDDEN DIMENSION OF EXECUTIVE DEVELOPMENT

On the surface, although the Executive MasterClass™ Program is structured much like a traditional 12-week course of study combining face-to-face learning with online learning, many of the similarities to traditional forms of teaching and learning end here. Every course requirement is based on relevant literature in the field of organizational development and change and is tightly coupled with application in practice. The gap between theory and its application to resolve pressing organizational issues often appears as a chasm to be spanned. Because this distinction appears to be maintained with fervor akin to the separation of church and state in many traditional academic settings, a central role of the facilitator is to act as a bridge between these two realms.

Bridging the realms of theory and practice is met with resistance from both sides of the divide. As the late Donald Schön (1983; 1987) pointed out, academics spend much of their lives being socialized to maintain the pristine character of theory, unsoiled by the often swampy and chaotic world of practice. On the other side of the divide, today's high-tech world epitomizes the impatient culture. The very idea of theory conjures visions of irrelevance and memories of late-adolescent struggles to stay awake in class. Students have little (if any) patience for the rigor of theoretical knowledge. What they want instead is a solution for their myriad problems to be solved yesterday.

*Praxis* is the term we have chosen to describe the bridging of the divide between theory and practice. From an ancient Greek term meaning *doing* and *action* – as well as *custom*, *habit*, and *manner* – the word is ideally suited to describe the relationship between our beliefs and behaviors. The term, as we use it here, connotes a need to critically examine, and when necessary to modify, the assumptions, customs, and beliefs that inform our practice. Praxis can thus be thought of as a dance between theory and practice, each realm informing and modifying the other in a seamless movement, thereby creating novel avenues for effective action. Viewed in this manner, neither theory nor practice is sufficient in and of itself; both realms must enlighten, enhance, and modify each other.

# CONCLUSION
# FIVE KEY OUTCOMES

At a time when many leaders report feeling overwhelmed by the complexity of their world, the results of the Executive MasterClass™ Program intervention suggest that there is a way through the maze. In this form of facilitated online Action-Learning, learning occurs when individuals and groups discover and narrow or eliminate gaps between intentions and results, between thoughts and actions, and between theories and practices. As we look back on our experience in this learning initiative, we can identify five key outcomes.

1. *Enhanced awareness of self.* Working in an online learning environment requires that participants articulate their thoughts, feelings, and perceptions in written form rather than reacting based on a sense of urgency and unconscious impulses. This environment enhances individual knowledge when participants become aware of, understand, and are able to explain the bases of their thoughts and actions.
2. *Enhanced awareness of others.* Because the work of all participants is viewed and commented on by the entire group, participants often learn from one another as much as they do from the program facilitator. In the earlier example, John drew extensively from the work of his directors in generating his own insights and intervention. Each participant also provided substantive feedback on others' initiatives. Thus, the thoughts and ideas of each participant are viewed from

multiple perspectives rather than from the relatively narrow view of the facilitator or teacher. In very concrete terms, participants learn that although their perspective may make perfect sense in terms of the operations of their respective organizational unit, it might not always make sense from the vantage point of the actions of several organizational units.

As one director commented,

> This has been eye-opening for me, being able to view other teams and people, understand their theories and how they operate. I see great opportunities to more easily and freely make course corrections as I become more aware of the company's operating theories. It has been nice to get to know the others on this team.

The last sentence in this director's comment is especially illuminating given that this was a team whose members had worked together closely for several years. Further testimony to the power of collaborative online learning to raise the level of awareness of self and others appears in the following commentaries:

> I'm still hesitant about sharing myself personally, but I feel myself becoming less shy. I'm learning new things to try as a manager and am gaining a greater appreciation of this team – our insights and knowledge.

> I am learning that the core of who I am is the foundation for how I act and react to the world around me. The ripple effect is phenomenal. I am struck by how open everyone is becoming and how free our self-expression is. I have gained a greater appreciation for everyone.

3. *Enhanced capacity for reflection.* Unlike purely verbal communication, the asynchronous learning environment also permits added time for reflection before response, giving the

dialogue a level of depth that is uncommon in other communication media. This capacity of the learning system thus enables participants to become aware of, more fully understand, and appreciate the thinking of others.

4. *New perspectives and knowledge.* The ability to weave multiple viewpoints together creates new knowledge and a broader perspective, thereby increasing *internal* coherence and *capacity* to initiate more effective and coordinated change initiatives.

5. *Enhanced capacity to initiate and sustain change.* Emerging out of the team's heightened awareness and new perspective; members were able to propose several new initiatives that have had a significant impact on the culture and operation of their organization. In addition, because those who would be affected by the change generated these initiatives in a structured and highly collaborative manner from their inception, resistance to implementation was greatly diminished.

We had the privilege of witnessing an awakening of spirit and seeing a growing sense of optimism emerge from an atmosphere previously blamed for extinguishing the vitality of those living within it. Hopelessness and helplessness faded as leaders once again were restored to a sense of confidence and capability. Most important, the intervention appeared to stimulate the ability of individual team members to collaborate on the design and implementation of organizational change initiatives as well as to lead those initiatives. We met with John several months after the conclusion of his teams' Executive MasterClass™ Program. The conversation covered a variety of issues related to our ongoing work together. In reflecting on the intervention and his heightened sense of awareness, John noted that the journey he was on was just beginning. His words have remained with us: "Once you've seen what we have had the chance to see, you can never go back."

# 13  CORPORATE AND HIGHER EDUCATION PRACTICES IN AN ACTION-LEARNING CONTEXT

*This chapter was reprinted with permission from (LaRue 2002)*

## THE 4-PLEX MODEL OF NETWORKED LEARNING

The specific components of the following model and their interaction emerged as the author observed the learning and development practices of professionals operating in geographically dispersed organizations (LaRue 1999). The model also emerged as a result of my work with graduate students performing their studies in a networked graduate school learning environment and applying their knowledge in a wide variety of public and private sector organizations. In addition, while not operating under the auspices of a university system, my colleagues and I continue to use these principles in our consulting practice, which focuses on executive and organization development in a variety of complex organizational settings. The major objectives of the 4-Plex Model of networked learning are as follows:

1. Provide the infrastructure for an expanded community of practice that transcends boundaries of particular organizations and rigid disciplinary domains.

2. Offer ready and timely access to an arena for theoretical discourse based on the mechanisms of cultural storage, dissemination, interchange, and creative addition.
3. Provide transferable credentials as well as a ready means for keeping these credentials current.
4. Carry out the preceding functions in a manner consistent with the geographic, time, and developmental demands of adult professionals.

To help in understanding this model graphically, I have included the following diagram:

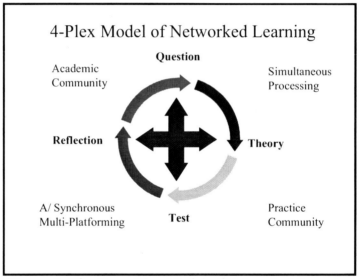

*Figure 8: The Four-Plex Model of Networked Learning*

The four main components of this model – question, theory, test, and reflection – are arranged in a matrix designed to indicate a nonlinear movement among each respective domain. The question and test (or vertical) dimension of the diagram is intended to represent the practice domain, and the reflection and theory (or horizontal) dimension is intended to represent the academic domain. That these two domains are joined by a common axis indicates a unification of the two fields, and their distinct quadrants represent their relative autonomy and distinct character. This aspect of the model is intended to directly address the need for the relevance of academic study to the arenas where workers apply their knowledge.

# QUESTION AND TEST DIMENSION: THE PRACTICE DOMAIN

The vertical axis represents the arena of what Schön (1987) refers to as the "swampy" zones of practice, wherein problematic situations are encountered. In this arena, questions arise, as do processes for evaluating the effectiveness of potential solutions. This dimension is designed to provide grounding for theory and a basis for evaluating the relevance of learning through its direct application in the workplace.

# REFLECTION AND THEORY: THE ACADEMIC DIMENSION

The horizontal dimension offers an arena for informing questions derived in the practice domain with relevant literature and research. It is also a domain of abstracted or "de-contextualized" thought and reflection that affords the chance to examine the problem from multiple critical perspectives. Theory also refers to theoretical reasoning and reflection based on the development of cognitive and epistemological competencies required for knowledge work.

# SIMULTANEOUS PROCESSING

All domains are accessible from all other points in the matrix at all times. Each domain can be used separately or simultaneously in both distal and local arenas. Both academic and practice arenas can be engaged simultaneously through appropriate technologies so that problems encountered at work can be reflected on in the academic environment and vice versa. This dimension of the model is designed to tighten and strengthen feedback loops between academia and complex modern work environments.

## A/SYNCHRONOUS MULTI-PLATFORMING

Work at any point (or among points) of the matrix can be accomplished by using any appropriate technological media in both synchronous and asynchronous modes. Such media include various network platforms, phone, fax, and e-mail used wherever and whenever as circumstances, time, and geographic proximity warrant. This dimension of the model is designed to address the need for greater mobility and flexibility in workforce learning through the leveraging of appropriate technologies.

## ACADEMIC COMMUNITY

This dimension refers to ready access to academic resources such as research libraries, networks, databases, journals, and books. It also includes communities of scholars, practitioners, and researchers engaged through college courses, degree programs, and related support services. This dimension of the model is designed to explicitly conceive of the university as an "infrastructure for expanded communities of practice" that extends beyond traditional practice arenas to encompass various academic disciplines, economic sectors, and social domains. It is expected that the academic community can be engaged either in physical face-to-face settings or at a distance via electronic means as circumstances warrant. This aspect of the model is also intended to address the need for increased mobility and time constraints of knowledge workers.

Quite often, the rapid pace and highly volatile character of many of today's organizational environments do not lend themselves to reflection and to inform actions through relevant theory embodied in academic (and other professional) research. The result is that many organizations inadvertently find themselves in the unenviable position of "reinventing the wheel" as they confront problematic issues that have been the subject of academic inquiry. Students and knowledge workers must be able to obtain the skills for locating and judging the relevance of research as it applies to their particular situations. Students must also become adept at making contributions to existing knowledge.

# PRACTICE COMMUNITY

The practice community refers to colleagues and team members within organizations and also includes professional networks outside of the organization. This dimension of the model is designed to address the workers' need for full engagement in professional networks as an integral component of their learning and developmental process. This dimension also addresses the need for learning accomplished outside the organization to be more relevant to the practice domain.

# EXAMPLE OF THE 4-PLEX MODEL IN ACTION

The central organizing principle of the model assumes that network technologies are, first and foremost, enablers of simultaneous functioning within all domains represented in the matrix. For example, a student who is also a member of an organization identifies a complex problem (or question) in his or her organization and attempts to generate a solution through dialogue with colleagues (reflection and practice community) through use of the company intranet, phone conferencing, face-to-face meetings, and so on (a/synchronous multi-platforms). Assuming that solutions are not forthcoming, dialogue concerning the problem extends to the Internet discussion groups, a conversation with peers, or a conference hosted by a professional association (professional networks).

As a participant in a university program, the problem can be addressed with peers in a course related to the subject. The student draws from the expertise of faculty and student peers (reflection and academic community) who work in other industries that may have dealt with a similar problem. The individual discovers a body of literature on the subject (theory) that can help him or her to understand the problem in a broader and more systemic context (theoretical reasoning). This process may, in turn, lead to a reframing of the problem as it is informed by relevant literature and further reflection with professional colleagues and peers.

Defining what now appears to be a suitable solution, the learner writes a proposal (submitted for credit in the academic community) for action to his or her company that is now informed by a broad array of resources. The plan is implemented on a pilot basis, and the next iteration of the cycle begins. Existing theory may be insufficient to describe the problematic phenomena, providing the student with an ideal opportunity to add to the body of literature on the subject through further research, theory building, testing, and reflection informed by an expansive array of colleagues and peers.

The central point of this model is that learning, enabled by the use of appropriate technologies, is now capable of occurring in both local and distal arenas simultaneously, with virtually seamless feedback between the domains of academia and practice. Network technologies are not viewed as mechanisms of delivery; instead, they are viewed as more or less transparent tools for dialogue and research. The core competencies of academia and business are also preserved, maintaining their respective autonomy while informing one another in a seamless flow of questioning, theorizing, testing, and reflecting, thereby re-conceptualizing the relationship among theory, learning, and practice.

# REFERENCES

Adizes, I. (1999). Managing corporate lifecycles. Paramus, N.J., Prentice Hall Press: xix, 460 p.

Allee, V. (1997). The knowledge evolution: Expanding organizational intelligence. Oxford, Butterworth-Heinemann.

Allee, V. (2003). The future of knowledge: increasing prosperity through value networks. Amsterdam; Boston, Butterworth-Heinemann.

Argyris, C. (1992). *On organization learning.* Cambridge, Blackwell Publishers.

Argyris, C. (1993). Knowledge for action: a guide to overcoming barriers to organizational change. San Francisco, Jossey-Bass.

Argyris, C. and D. Schön (1996). *Organization learning II: Theory, method, and practice.* New York, Addison-Wesley.

Axelrod, R. M. and M. D. Cohen (1999). Harnessing complexity: organizational implications of a scientific frontier. New York, Free Press.

Bateson, G. (1979). *Mind and nature: a necessary unity.* New York, Dutton.

Beck D. and Cowan C. (1995) Spiral Dynamics: mastering values, leadership, and change. Malden, Mass. Blackwell Publishing, Inc.

Bennis, W. G. and P. W. Biederman (1997). *Organizing genius: the secret of creative collaboration.* Reading, Mass., Addison-Wesley.

Bion, W. R. (1961). *Experiences in groups, and other papers.* New York, Basic Books.

Bohm, D. (1994). *Thought as a system.* London; New York, Routledge.

Bohm, D. and L. Nichol (1996). *On dialogue.* London; New York, Routledge.

Brown, J. S. and P. Duguid (2000). *The social life of information.* Boston, Harvard Business School Press.

Brown, J. S. and P. Duguid (2002). *The social life of information.* Boston, Harvard Business School Press.

Capra, F. (2002). The hidden connections: integrating the biological, cognitive, and social dimensions of life into a science of sustainability. New York, Doubleday.

Carter, L., D. Giber, et al. (2000). Linkage, Inc.'s best practices in organization & human resources development handbook: case studies - instruments - models - research. Lexington, MA, Linkage Press.

Collins, J. C. (2001). Good to great: why some companies make the leap--and others don't. New York, NY, HarperBusiness.

Davenport, T. H. and L. Prusak (1998). *Working knowledge: how organizations manage what they know.* Boston, Mass, Harvard Business School Press.

Dewey, J. (1916). Democracy and education. New York, Institute for Learning Technologies: Columbia University. 1998.

Drucker, P. F. (1999). *Management challenges for the 21st century.* New York, HarperBusiness: xi, 207 p.

Drucker, P. F. (1999). *Management challenges for the 21st century.* New York, HarperBusiness.

Drucker, P. F. (2002). *Managing in the next society.* New York, St. Martin's Press.

Fulmer, R. M. and M. Goldsmith (2001). The leadership investment: how the world's best organizations gain strategic advantage through leadership development. New York, AMACOM.

Goldsmith, M. (2003). *The many facets of leadership.* Upper Saddle River, NJ, Financial Times/Prentice Hall.

Goldsmith, M., L. Lyons, et al. (2000). Coaching for leadership: how the world's greatest coaches help leaders learn. San Francisco, Jossey Bass/Pfeiffer.

Goldsmith, M., H. J. Morgan, et al. (2004). *Leading organizational learning: harnessing the power of knowledge.* San Francisco, Calif., Jossey-Bass.

Goleman, D., R. E. Boyatzis, et al. (2002). Primal leadership: realizing the power of emotional intelligence. Boston, Mass., Harvard Business School Press: xvii, 306 p.

Gould, S. J. (2000). The Spice of Life: An Interview with Stephen Jay Gould. *Leader to Leader* 15 (Winter 2000): 14-19.

Griffin, D. and R. D. Stacey (2005). *Complexity and the experience of leading organizations.* New York, Routledge.

Hersey, P. (1985). *The situational leader.* New York, NY, Warner Books.

Hesselbein, F., M. Goldsmith, et al. (1996). The leader of the future: new visions, strategies, and practices for the next era. San Francisco, Jossey-Bass.

Hock, D. (1999). *Birth of the chaordic age.* San Francisco, Berrett-Koehler Publishers.

Hock, D. (2000). The Art of Chaordic Leadership. *Leader to Leader.* Winter 2000(15): 20-26.

Johnson, S. (2001). Emergence: the connected lives of ants, brains, cities, and software. New York, Scribner.

Kauffman, S. A. (1995). At home in the universe: the search for laws of self-organization and complexity. New York, Oxford University Press.

Kegan, R. (1994). *In over our heads: the mental demands of modern life.* Cambridge, Mass., Harvard University Press.

Kegan, R. and L. L. Lahey (2001). How the way we talk can change the way we work: seven languages for transformation. San Francisco, Jossey-Bass.

Kleiner, A. and G. Roth (1998). How to make experience your company's best teacher. *Harvard Business Review on knowledge management.* Boston, MA, Harvard Business School Press: 137-152.

Kotter, J. P. (1996). *Leading change.* Boston, Mass., Harvard Business School Press.

Kotter, J. P. (1999). *John P. Kotter on what leaders really do.* Boston, Harvard Business School Press.

Kotter, J. P. and D. S. Cohen (2002). *The heart of change: real-life stories of how people change their organizations.* Boston, Mass., Harvard Business School Press.

LaRue, B. (1999). Toward a unified view of working, living and learning in the knowledge economy: Implications of the new learning imperative for distributed organizations, higher education and knowledge workers._Human and Organization Development.* Santa Barbara, CA, The Fielding Institute.

LaRue, B. (2002). Synthesizing higher education and corporate learning strategies. Handbook of online learning: innovations in higher education and corporate training. J. Schoenholtz-Read. Thousand Oaks, Calif., Sage Publications.

LaRue, B. (2005). Action Leaders: Action-Learning at the Top. *Leadership Excellence, 22:12.*

LaRue, B. (2005). Getting Things Done Through Action-Learning Teams. *Leadership Excellence: 18.*

LaRue, B. (2005). Soft Focus: The New Edge of Mastery. *Personal Excellence.*

LaRue, B. and R. Ivany (2004). Transform Your Culture Through Action-Learning Teams. *Executive Excellence:* 14-15.

LaRue, B. and M. Sobol (2002). The Executive Master Class: Cyberspace and the New Frontiers of Executive Education. *Handbook of online learning: innovations in higher education and corporate training.* J. Schoenholtz-Read. Thousand Oaks, Calif., Sage Publications.

Lave, J. and E. Wenger (1991). *Situated learning: legitimate peripheral participation.* Cambridge England; New York, Cambridge University Press.

Lesser, E. L. (2000). Knowledge and social capital: foundations and applications. Boston, Butterworth-Heinemann.

Lesser, E. L., M. A. Fontaine, et al. (2000). *Knowledge and communities.* Boston, Butterworth-Heinemann.

Lesser, E. L. and L. Prusak (2004). Creating value with knowledge: insights from the IBM institute for business value. Oxford ; New York, Oxford University Press.

McKinsey and Company. *The McKinsey quarterly.* [New York,, McKinsey & Co.]: v.

McMaster, M. (1996). The intelligence advantage: Organizing for complexity. London, Butterworth-Heinemann.

Meril, R., S. Covey, et al. (1994). *First things first.* New York, Simon and Schuster.

Mitleton-Kelly, E. (2001). The Principles of Complexity and Enabling Infrastructures. In *Complex Systems and Evolutionary Perspectives of Organizations: The Application of Complexity Theory to Organizations.* London, London School of Economics.

Morgan, G. (1997). *Images of organization,* Thousand Oaks, Calif., Sage Publications.

Morgan, G. (1997). *Images of organization.* Thousand Oaks, Calif., Sage Publications.

Nonaka, I. and T. Nishiguchi (2001). Knowledge emergence: social, technical, and evolutionary dimensions of knowledge creation. Oxford ; New York, Oxford University Press.

Nonaka, I. and H. Takeuchi (1995). The knowledge creating company: How Japanese companies create the dynamics of innovation. Oxford, Oxford University Press.

Piaget, J. (1977). *Epistemology and psychology of functions.* Dordrecht; Boston, D. Reidel Pub. Co.

Prahalad, C. K. and V. Ramaswamy (2004). *The future of competition: co-creating unique value with customers.* Boston, Mass., Harvard Business School Pub.

Rothwell, W. J. (1999). The action learning guidebook: a real-time strategy for problem solving, training design, and employee development. San Francisco, Jossey-Bass/Pfeiffer.

Saint-Onge, H. and D. Wallace (2003). *Leveraging communities of practice for strategic advantage.* Amsterdam ; Boston, Butterworth-Heinemann.

Schön, D. (1983). *The Reflective Practitioner.* New York, Basic Books.

Schön, D. (1987). Educating the reflective practitioner: Toward a new design for teaching and learning in the professions. San Francisco, Jossey-Bass.

Segil, L., M. Goldsmith, et al. (2003). *Partnering: the new face of leadership.* New York, AMACOM.

Senge, P. (1990). The fifth discipline: The art and practice of the learning organization. New York, Doubleday.

Senge, P., Ed. (1994). The fifth discipline field book: Strategies and tools for building a learning organization. New York, Doubleday.

Senge, P. M. (1999). The dance of change: the challenges of sustaining momentum in learning organizations. New York, Currency/Doubleday.

Stacey, R. D. (2001). Complex responsive processes in organizations: learning and knowledge creation. London; New York, Routledge.

Stacey, R. D. (2003). *Strategic management and organizational dynamics: the challenge of complexity.* Harlow, England; New York, Prentice Hall/Financial Times.

Stacey, R. D. and D. Griffin (2005). A complexity perspective on researching organizations: taking experience seriously. London; New York, Routledge.

Takeuchi, H. and I. Nonaka (2004). *Hitotsubashi on knowledge management.* Singapore, John Wiley & Sons (Asia).

Task Force on High-Performance Work and Workers (1997). Spanning the chasm: Corporate and academic cooperation to improve work-force preparation. Washington D.C., Business-Higher Education Forum in affiliation with the American Council on Education.

Tsoukas, H. (2005). Complex knowledge: studies in organizational epistemology. New York, Oxford University Press.

Tsoukas, H. and N. Mylonopoulos (2004). Organizations as knowledge systems: knowledge, learning, and dynamic capabilities. New York, Palgrave Macmillan.

Tsoukas, H. and J. Shepherd (2004). *Managing the future : foresight in the knowledge economy.* Malden, MA, USA, Blackwell Pub.

Tsoukas, H., C. Knudsen, et al. (2003). *The Oxford handbook of organization theory.* Oxford; New York, Oxford University Press.

Tsoukas, H. (1994). New thinking in organizational behaviour: from social engineering to reflective action. Oxford; Boston, Butterworth-Heinemann.

Tuomi, I. (2002). *Networks of innovation: change and meaning in the age of the Internet.* Oxford, England; New York, Oxford University Press.

Vygotsky, L. (1986). *Thought and language.* Cambridge, MA, MIT Press.
Waldrop, M. M. (1992). *Complexity: the emerging science at the edge of order and chaos.* New York, Simon & Schuster.

Wenger, E. (1998). *Communities of practice: learning, meaning, and identity.* Cambridge, U.K.; New York, N.Y., Cambridge University Press.

Wenger, E., R. A. McDermott, et al. (2002). *Cultivating communities of practice: a guide to managing knowledge.* Boston, Mass., Harvard Business School Press.

Wilber, K. (2001). *Quantum questions : mystical writings of the world's great physicists.* Boston, [New York], Shambhala; Distributed in the U.S. by Random House.

Zuboff, S. (1988). In the age of the smart machine: The future of work and power. New York, Basic Books.

# ABOUT THE AUTHORS

## BRUCE LARUE, PH.D.

Dr. Bruce LaRue is President of Applied Development Services, Inc., a consultancy specializing in executive and organization development. Bruce has focused much of his career on the emergence of the knowledge economy and its implications for the development of leadership competencies in distributed, technologically complex organizations. He has proven to be a gifted facilitator of action learning seminars for executives and their teams. As teacher and coach, his quietly confident manner tends to bring out the best in people personally and professionally, and he has a reputation for inspiring fresh approaches to learning and change in the workplace.

In 1996, Bruce was appointed Associate Fellow of the World Academy of Art and Science by former NATO Ambassador Harlan Cleveland to research The Future of Work. Bruce has taught at the University of Washington Tacoma, and is a member of the faculty of the Adizes Graduate School. He taught at The Fielding Graduate University, where he completed his doctorate in Human and Organizational Systems. He also regularly serves on the faculty of the Global Institute for Leadership Development.

Bruce recently presented at Linkage's Next Generation Leadership summit in Orlando Florida with Major General Robert Ivany, former President of the U.S. Army War College. An article based on this talk appears in the December 2004 issue of Leadership Excellence Magazine, where Bruce is a regular contributor.

Bruce recently served as a senior organizational consultant on the Boeing 777-LR World Tour project,, showcasing the latest 777 and

787 Dreamliner interior concepts at the Paris Airshow in June 2005.

As a consultant and professor, Bruce has worked with managers and executives in aerospace, the Department of Defense, telecommunications, network technologies, pharmaceuticals, petrochemicals, financial services, municipal government, and the non-profit sector.

**Contact:**
Phone: (253) 576-7100
E-Mail: bruce@brucelarue.com
Web: www.brucelarue.com

# PAUL CHILDS

In addition to *"Leading Organizations from the Inside Out"*, Paul has penned numerous articles on leadership and organizational transformation. He served as the Vice President for the Adizes Institute for Organizational Change and as the Editor of Insights, the monthly Adizes Newsletter.

Dr. Adizes pioneered the principals of organizational lifecycles. Paul developed trainings and systems to market and license this work to companies. He developed new methods for producing culture change and restructuring companies in transition along with Dr. Adizes.

Paul Childs was the founder and Managing Partner of Summit Corporate Partners, a regional investment bank and CEO of Century Data Products, a mainframe computer parts supplier.

Paul presently chairs an Advisory Board of business owners, company presidents and CEOs for TEC International, the oldest and largest organization of Chief Executives. He is also the managing partner for Provarus, a strategic consulting firm that focuses on breaking limiting patterns of behavior for high performing organizations and executives in transition.

His clients have included the US Navy, Applied Materials, Pacific Bell, AT&T, Digital Equipment Corporation, Xcyte Therapies (a public biotech firm), UIEvolution (a software company founded by the principal software architect for Bill Gates and Microsoft.), and countless entrepreneurial companies both public and private.

His workshop *"Business Mastery for Entrepreneurs"* was designed to break the Entrepreneur's Trap and has been taught worldwide in Los Angeles, London, New York, Spain, and Mexico. In London, graduates have formed the Business Mastery Alliance, a group of high performing companies, to continue the principals learned in the work and to encourage others to break limiting patterns in their enterprises.

Paul spent several years as an executive coach and trainer for Anthony Robbins. As a certified NLP trainer, Paul shares this additional unique knowledge base with his high performing executive clients through personal coaching. Paul is also certified in Marshall Goldsmith's Behavioral Coaching method and was a member of Marshall's group Association for Strategic Leadership. Paul is also a member of the Association for Strategic Growth; the Turnaround Management Association and the Association for Corporate Growth.

Paul received his Bachelors Degree in Business Management from Antioch University. He is currently pursuing a Masters of Business Administration from Pepperdine University.

He is also an accomplished jazz pianist and has lived in Oak Park California for the last 13 years where he tries to balance his work life with his real passion, his family: his beautiful wife Ulyssa and their three boys Jordan, Tobin and Ethan.

**Contact:**
Phone: (818) 515-5558
E-Mail: pchilds@provarus.com

# KERRY LARSON, PH.D.

Dr. Kerry Larson is a co-founder of Provarus Group, a consulting firm that specializes in Organizational Transformation and Change Management.

Kerry is an experienced senior executive with an extensive background in organizational development and executive coaching. During twenty-five years working with senior executives individually and in teams, he has won a reputation for effectiveness as a coach and mentor, with an intuitive skill for assessing individual talent and organizational needs.

Kerry has a gift for building trust and a record for delivering practical results. Having worked successfully with organizations through rapid growth, mergers, crises and turnarounds, he knows how to inspire others towards positive change.

Kerry's ability to create powerful work environments is rooted in executive leadership experience. While he was Senior Vice President for People Development at AT&T Wireless, it was named best large company to work for by CEO magazine for three years running. He has also been a Senior Vice President at McCaw Communications, and Vice President at Teledesic and Avia International.

Before helping to found Leadership Strategies International, Kerry was Senior Consultant with RHR (Rohrer, Hibler, and Replogle), an international consulting firm of organizational psychologists. He has consulted with a number of organizations including AT&T, Nextlink, Nextel Partners, Teledesic, Bank of Hawaii, Willamette Industries, Tacoma News Tribune, Ignition, Think Share, Microvision, and is a valued member of a number of advisory boards.

With a Ph.D. in psychology, Kerry has taught at the University of Utah, North Texas University, Brigham Young University, and Virginia Tech.

**Contact:**
Phone: (425) 830-8618
E-Mail: kerrybl@comcast.net